The Hotel Room

A Comedy Play

Ashley Burgoyne

Copyright © Ashley Burgoyne 2020

ashleyburgoyne.wixsite.com/writerandcomposer

ashleyburgoynewriter@gmail.com

First Edition published in 2020

Updated in 2022

All rights whatsoever in this play are strictly reserved and applications for permission to perform it, etc., must be made in advance, before rehearsals begin, direct to the author at ashleyburgoynewriter@gmail.com

ISBN: 9798610633916

No one shall make any changes in this title for the purpose of production. No part of this book may be reproduced, stored in a retrieval system, or transmitted in any form, by any means, now known or yet to be invented, including mechanical, electronic, photocopying, recording, videotaping, or otherwise, without the prior written permission of the author. No one shall upload this title, or part of this title, to any social media websites

THE HOTEL ROOM

First presented at The Little Theatre by the Park, Chesham, Bucks on 23rd June 2022 by Phoenix Players Chesham, with the following cast:

Andrew	John Jensen
Susan	Jen Smyth
Megan	Cathrine Platts
Trish	Hilary Brown
George	Alex Micallef
Caroline	Jacinta Blackburn
Olivia	Carla van de Sluijs
Dallas	Ryan McGregor
Claire	Eleanor Phillips
Peter	Jonathan Coburn

Directed by Helen Salisbury and Jane Dodd

Characters

Andrew	40s
Susan	40s, Andrew's wife
Megan	40s-50s, Chambermaid
Trish	40s-50s, Chambermaid
George	60s, Andrew's boss
Caroline	60s, George's wife
Olivia	20s, George and Caroline's granddaughter
Dallas	20s, Olivia's boyfriend
Claire	70s, Andrew's mother
Peter	70s, Andrew's father

ACT 1

Scene 1

A hotel room. 7:15pm.
The room is quite unspectacular, with décor which is past its best and due an update. Upstage, centre, is a freshly made-up double bed with a small bedside table each side. Each table has a lamp upon it. One table has the customary Bible upon it. Downstage there is a small dressing table and stool. One side of the stage is the exit to the bathroom. Near to this exit is a small table with the usual kettle and two cups and saucers, etc. The other side of the stage is the door leading onto the hotel corridor. In, through this door, enters Susan followed by Andrew, both in their forties. They are both casually dressed and rather tired. Andrew is carrying two small overnight bags, whilst Susan has her handbag.

ANDREW   There you go. Made it!

SUSAN   *(collapsing onto the bed and closing her eyes)* Finally!

ANDREW   *(placing one bag next to Susan's side of the bed and walking round to the other side to place his own)* What do you think?

SUSAN   *(neither looking up, or opening her eyes)* Mmmm?

ANDREW   The room? What do you think?

SUSAN   *(slowly sitting up and opening her eyes)* Oh, yes, the room. Lovely.

ANDREW   And to think it all started here…

SUSAN   Sorry?

ANDREW   My parents. Their honeymoon, their life, all started here.

SUSAN   *(looking around unconvincingly)* Yes. It was nice of them to recommend it. *(Pause)* Do you think it was like this back then?

ANDREW   What do you mean?

SUSAN Well, it doesn't really come across as a honeymoon kind of hotel, does it?

ANDREW No?

SUSAN No.

ANDREW *(looking around)* No. I suppose it doesn't really. Maybe it was nicer back then.

SUSAN Maybe.

ANDREW Yes.

SUSAN Or maybe it was the same.

ANDREW Eh?

SUSAN I mean I don't think it's been redecorated.

ANDREW What! In nearly 50 years?

SUSAN Yes!

ANDREW *(looking around once more)* Oh dear. You could be right. *(Sitting on the bed next to Susan. Pause)* Sorry.

SUSAN What for?

ANDREW All this.

SUSAN It's hardly your fault that they haven't decorated for half a century, is it?

ANDREW No. But when my parents offered to have the twins…

SUSAN Sorry. What was that, Andrew?

ANDREW I said 'when my parents offered to have the twins…'

SUSAN *(interrupting)* I know what you said; but we've had this discussion before. It's either Samuel and Eleanor, or the children. Not the twins.

ANDREW Yes, I know…

SUSAN As I've said on many an occasion; they are individuals.

ANDREW Yes, but…

SUSAN Apart from their nappies, which happen to be the same make, they are individuals. From Babygro to bonnet.

ANDREW *(conceding defeat)* Yes.

SUSAN Or, in Samuel's case; cap.

ANDREW Yes. Sorry.

SUSAN You were saying?

ANDREW What? Oh, yes. When my parents offered to have *the children*, and I said that that would be nice, but that I didn't know where to take you and they suggested here… I, well, I just felt that I should book here seeing as they'd offered to babysit and often talked of how wondrous this hotel was and…

SUSAN And what?

ANDREW Oh, I don't know. I stupidly thought that some old-fashioned romance might rub off on us a bit.

SUSAN *(rubbing Andrew's arm)* That's not stupid. You never know, it might!

ANDREW But the room seems less of the romance and more of the old-fashioned!

SUSAN Then we'll just have to work on the romance, won't we?

ANDREW That'd be nice. I just wish I'd got us better surroundings.

SUSAN Never mind. We'll make do. We always do.

ANDREW I know we always do. *(Getting up and heading to the window – front of stage)* I just wish I'd booked us somewhere better. I should have guessed it had gone downhill, seeing as it's only a two-star hotel. My

	parents remembered it as a four-star hotel.
SUSAN	It doesn't matter. It's sentimental to your parents. And at least it's not a one-star hotel!
ANDREW	*(smiling)* True. Although, I don't think I've ever seen a one-star hotel…
SUSAN	What's the view like?
ANDREW	*(looking out of the window)* Not bad. As long as you look beyond the car park. There's a bit of a view in between the two buildings opposite.
SUSAN	Lovely. *(Pause)* What time did you book dinner for?
ANDREW	They said that we needed to order our food before 8, so I went for 7:45. *(Looking at his watch)* So that gives us, what, 25 minutes before we should head down.
SUSAN	Ok. *(Looking down at her casual dress)* Do you think we need to dress for dinner?
ANDREW	I shouldn't think so. I glanced in the dining room on the way up and it didn't look like anyone was particularly smart.
SUSAN	Ok.
ANDREW	Unless you want to?
SUSAN	Mmmm?
ANDREW	Well, I mean, I know it's only two-star and no one else appears to have dressed for dinner *(sitting on the bed next to Susan)* but, you can dress for dinner if you fancy a change. After all this is a change, isn't it? *(Taking her hand)* Me and you, away together, no children, for the first time in four years.
SUSAN	Yes, it is. Isn't it. Maybe I should get changed.
ANDREW	It's up to you.
SUSAN	No, you're right. I'll get changed. *(Picking up her bag)*

Are you getting changed too?

ANDREW *(picking up his bag)* I'll pop a shirt on.

SUSAN Lovely. I need a wee, so I'll get changed in the bathroom.

ANDREW *(passing her his wash bag)* Can you pop this in there for me, please?

SUSAN *(taking it)* Sure. Won't be long. *(She exits to the bathroom)*

Pause

ANDREW *(changing his shirt and raising his voice so he's heard)* It's amazing, isn't it?

SUSAN What is?

ANDREW The fact that it's been four years since we've been away together.

SUSAN Yes, it is, isn't it.

ANDREW Time flies when you're....

Pause

SUSAN Having fun?

ANDREW Yes. That's it.

SUSAN *(sticking her head back into the room)* Some of it's been fun, hasn't it?

ANDREW *(looking up at her)* Of course it has. It's just....

SUSAN Just what?

ANDREW Just sometimes difficult to remember the fun stuff through the vast amounts of dirty nappies and vomit!

SUSAN *(laughing and returning to the bathroom)* At least you get to go to work.

ANDREW True.

SUSAN I have that all day long.

ANDREW Surely not.

SUSAN It's true!

ANDREW I don't believe that.

SUSAN It *is* true.

ANDREW It can't be.

SUSAN Why not?

ANDREW Because it's surely impossible for two tiny humans to excrete and throw up the amount they do when I'm at home and still have more to give you when I'm at work!

SUSAN *(returning from the bathroom, laughing)* They do!

ANDREW *(pausing to look at her)* Look at you!

SUSAN What about me?

ANDREW You look beautiful.

SUSAN Don't be silly.

ANDREW I'm not being silly. You look beautiful.

SUSAN I don't. I look like a forty-something year-old woman who's got two very young children and who is too old for this dress.

ANDREW *(walking towards her and taking her hand)* Now who's the one being silly, eh?

SUSAN Oh, you're so sweet, Andrew.

ANDREW If I say you're beautiful; then you're beautiful. Ok?

SUSAN Ok. I just wish I felt it!

ANDREW Come here. *(They hug)* We've got 18 hours alone together. We can have a nice meal, a bottle of wine, a soak in the bath. I can give you a lovely massage; I haven't done that for years, have I? Then we can dim the lights and...

During the above, since 18 hours was mentioned, Susan, whilst hugging, has been looking at her watch and counting her fingers

SUSAN *(interrupting)* 18?

ANDREW Pardon?

SUSAN *(standing apart)* You said 18 hours.

ANDREW Yes.

SUSAN That can't be right. *(Counting her fingers again)* That's far too long!

ANDREW What do you mean?

SUSAN I mean that 18 hours is far too long!

ANDREW *(walking away, quite disgruntled)* Well; after waiting over four years I'd have thought that 18 hours was the least...

SUSAN *(following and interrupting)* No, no. *(Taking his hands)* I don't mean that 18 hours is too long with you.

ANDREW Oh, right, good!

SUSAN No, I meant that 18 hours is too long to leave the children with your parents.

ANDREW Oh, right. *(Pause)* Is it?

SUSAN Yes.

ANDREW But this whole trip has come about because they offered to take the children overnight.

SUSAN Yes, I know, and it's very sweet of them, but they did say to collect the children at 11 in the morning.

ANDREW No they didn't. They said from 11.

SUSAN Same thing.

ANDREW Well it's not really.

SUSAN Isn't it?

ANDREW No. Collecting them at 11 means getting up early, having breakfast early and leaving here before 9. Whereas from 11 means have a lie-in, a late breakfast and leave late morning.

SUSAN We can't do that.

ANDREW We can. The last thing mum said to me was 'we don't mind if you're back at 3 or 4!'

SUSAN Did she?

ANDREW Yes!

SUSAN We can't do that.

ANDREW Why not?

SUSAN Because, well, for starters, it'll finish off your dad.

ANDREW *(laughing)* No it won't.

SUSAN And... oh no!

ANDREW What?!

SUSAN They won't have enough food! *(Becoming frantic)* I only left them enough for tonight and breakfast!

ANDREW *(trying to calm her down)* They'll be fine.

SUSAN No they won't. They'll starve!

ANDREW *(taking hold of her shoulders)* Now calm down. You know they won't starve. Mum and D... Mum'll look after them. She can cook, you know?!

SUSAN   *(calming down a little)* I know she can. It's just that the children sort of only like certain foods and they have their favourites. You know?

ANDREW   I know. But maybe they'll discover new foods and new favourites.

SUSAN   Maybe.

ANDREW   See.

SUSAN   Or, maybe they'll starve.

ANDREW   *(a little exasperated)* They won't starve!

SUSAN   If we get back for 11, it won't matter either way, will it?

ANDREW   Look. My mum did bring up four children of her own.

SUSAN   I know.

ANDREW   And we all turned out alright, didn't we?

SUSAN   Well….

ANDREW   Well, apart from Michael.

SUSAN   Yes.

ANDREW   And that wasn't Mum's fault.

SUSAN   No?

ANDREW   Well, not completely.

SUSAN   No.

ANDREW   It was obviously half Dad's fault… *(rushing on)* but, anyway, to misquote Meat Loaf; three out of four ain't bad!

SUSAN   *(smiling)* Ok. So, they won't starve. But I'd still prefer to pick them up before lunchtime tomorrow, please?

ANDREW   If that's what you want, then ok. But, how about we

	make the decision in the morning. See how we feel then. Ok?
SUSAN	Ok.
ANDREW	Right, *(offering his arm)* shall we dine, milady?
SUSAN	*(picking up her handbag and taking his arm)* Certainly, kind sir!

They exit. The stage is empty for at least 30 seconds. They return. A flustered Susan is followed by an exasperated Andrew

SUSAN	*(sitting on the bed and starting to rummage through her handbag)* I'm sorry, Andrew.
ANDREW	*(clearly disgruntled, but trying to keep himself in check)* It doesn't matter, Sue.
SUSAN	It does. How embarrassing. I'm sorry.
ANDREW	It's fine.
SUSAN	How can it be. Standing in the lift with four other people. Perfect strangers.
ANDREW	It's ok. *(Heading towards her and trying to calm her down)*
SUSAN	That dreadfully loud muzak playing…
ANDREW	Yes, well, that was dreadful.
SUSAN	…and loud…
ANDREW	Yes; and loud.
SUSAN	…and on the way to the restaurant I manage to shout…
ANDREW	It's ok.
SUSAN	…over the muzak…
ANDREW	Yes, well, you did well to be louder than that.

SUSAN *(shouting)* 'Microwave!'

ANDREW Yes.

Pause. Susan starts to gently cry as she extracts a tissue from her handbag. Andrew sits next to her on the bed

SUSAN *(quietly)* Sorry.

ANDREW *(equally quietly)* It doesn't matter.

Pause

SUSAN It does. I don't seem to be able to help myself, these days.

ANDREW It's ok.

SUSAN But in a small lift, with four other people sardined in with us? How embarrassing.

ANDREW *(vainly clutching at straws)* Yes; but it doesn't matter as I'm sure you'll never see them again.

SUSAN I suppose. *(Pause)* Sorry. It's only been happening since I've had the children.

ANDREW I know.

SUSAN What do you mean you know?

ANDREW I mean I know it's only been happening since we've had the children.

SUSAN You mean that I've blurted things out in front of you before.

ANDREW Yes.

SUSAN I hadn't realised that. I always thought I was out of your earshot.

ANDREW I'm afraid not.

SUSAN *(blowing her nose)* Go on then. What have you heard?

ANDREW   Apart from the one when we were shopping?

SUSAN   What one when we were shopping?

ANDREW   In Lidl, a couple of months ago.

SUSAN   Oh. You heard that one.

ANDREW   Well, I was with you at the time.

SUSAN   But I thought you were down the freezer aisle getting the sweetcorn when it happened.

ANDREW   I was.

SUSAN   *(in disbelief)* My God! You heard it all the way down there?

ANDREW   Afraid so.

SUSAN   Why didn't you tell me you'd heard it?

ANDREW   Well, I guessed that you were embarrassed enough without me bringing it up.

SUSAN   I was.

ANDREW   The fact that you hollered 'breast milk' at the top of your voice in Lidl is probably something you don't need reminding of.

SUSAN   No.

ANDREW   No.

SUSAN   A sympathetic member of staff did direct me towards the powdered baby milk, though!

ANDREW   Oh. That was nice of them.

SUSAN   Yes. You see I'd forgotten to express that morning and…

ANDREW   It's ok.

SUSAN	What else have you heard me blurt out?
ANDREW	Oh, I can't remember. Not much. I think you shouted 'washing' once, when you were in the shower.
SUSAN	That would've been the running water jogging my memory to do the washing.
ANDREW	Right. Erm… 'kitchen shelves'.
SUSAN	Kitchen shelves… kitchen shelves… There's usually a trigger…Oh, yes. I was watching 'Homes Under The Hammer' and 'hammer' reminded me that the kitchen shelves needed fixing.
ANDREW	Right.

Pause

Anyway; shouting 'microwave' in a tiny lift probably got those other guests thinking!

SUSAN	Sorry?
ANDREW	On our way to dine? They probably thought you were hoping for a microwave meal! Or, maybe they thought that you were suggesting the lift was the size of a microwave!
SUSAN	*(smiling)* Sorry.
ANDREW	So, why 'microwave'?
SUSAN	The children.
ANDREW	What?
SUSAN	The children. Their dinner.
ANDREW	What about it?
SUSAN	I didn't leave any instructions on how long to warm it up in the microwave for.
ANDREW	And that's it?

SUSAN Yes.

ANDREW All that embarrassment for that?!

SUSAN Yes, well, we were going for dinner. That must have triggered something in my head with regards to the children's dinners and as I thought it, I said it!

ANDREW I know.

SUSAN I'm sorry. I don't seem to be able to help myself.

ANDREW No. Do you want to go and see the doctor about it?

SUSAN Oh no.

ANDREW Are you sure? I mean I can come along with you. You know, for support.

SUSAN *(holding his hand)* That's very sweet of you, Andrew. But I think I'm just over tired. You know. Having twins and everything.

ANDREW Children.

SUSAN Pardon?

ANDREW Having children. You said 'having twins'.

SUSAN *(raising her voice slightly)* Yes, I meant having twins!

ANDREW But I thought…

SUSAN *(interrupting)* In this case I can say twins because I'm referring to the physical action of giving birth to two humans only seven minutes apart!

ANDREW Oh, right. I see.

SUSAN Good.

ANDREW I can see that could be quite taxing.

SUSAN Well, yes, not the word I would have used; but you could say that!

ANDREW   Ok. *(Pause)* What do you want to do about this microwave issue?

SUSAN   Phone your parents.

ANDREW   Really, Sue?

SUSAN   Yes. Why? Don't you want to check they're ok?

ANDREW   It's not that. It's the fact that you think my parents wouldn't be able to warm their food up properly in the microwave.

SUSAN   *(retrieving her mobile phone from her handbag)* Let's not argue, please, Andrew. Can you just phone them, please?

ANDREW   And say what?

SUSAN   *(slightly sarcastically)* That you want to know if Samuel and Eleanor are ok!

ANDREW   *(taking the phone)* I know that. I just don't want them to think that I'm checking up on them.

SUSAN   You'll be alright. Just phone them please.

ANDREW   *(punching numbers into the phone)* Ok. Now, no interrupting, please.

SUSAN   What do you mean?

ANDREW   You always interrupt me when I'm on the phone to my parents.

SUSAN   No I don't, it's you who interrupts me when I'm on the phone, I never…

ANDREW   *(holding his hand up as the phone is answered. Into phone)* Hi Dad. How are you…… good……coping alright with Sam 'n' Ella?……Oh, ok.

SUSAN   What's wrong?

ANDREW	*(holding his hand up)* Ok, yes, put Mum on...... bye, Dad.
SUSAN	What is it, Andrew?
ANDREW	*(waving his hand)* Hi Mum. Dad says you've just been putting the children to bed.
SUSAN	*(looking at her watch)* Just been putting them to bed! They should have been put to bed forty-five minutes ago!
ANDREW	*(staring at Susan)* Oh, I see... you were both reading them a bedtime story!
SUSAN	Oh, no. Not that story which is too old for them.
ANDREW	*(into phone)* Oh, I see. Don't you think that story's a bit too old for them?
SUSAN	Oh, God! It was that story, again!
ANDREW	*(into phone)* Well, yes, I know they are older than when you last read it to them, but only by three or four months.... Yes, well, I think they need to be quite a bit older, really!
SUSAN	Good grief.
ANDREW	*(into phone)* Yes, well, I know it's not the same story you read to Michael.... But it does have similarities....
SUSAN	*(putting her head in her hands)* God, give me strength!
ANDREW	*(continuing into phone)* Yes, well, is everything else ok?
SUSAN	Ask about the microwave, please, Andrew.
ANDREW	*(cupping the phone)* Yes, I will. *(Into phone)* Good.... Erm, Sue doesn't think she left you any instructions on how long to warm the children's dinner in the microwave for.... She didn't, right....
SUSAN	And?

ANDREW *(holding his hand up at Susan, again)* So, every 20 seconds you did what?

SUSAN *(starting to panic)* What?

ANDREW *(into phone)* You checked it.

SUSAN How?

ANDREW *(into phone)* How?.... Dad dipped what in it?

SUSAN God. I hope he says thermometer!

ANDREW *(into phone)* His little finger. Right.

SUSAN *(as she puts her hands over her mouth)* Oh, no. That's disgusting!

ANDREW *(into phone)* And after three dips it was done....

SUSAN I should think it was!

ANDREW *(into phone)* Lovely. Well I hope they sleep through for you....

SUSAN They'll probably never wake up now!

ANDREW *(glaring at Susan. Into phone)* I'll call you in the morning, when we're about to set off.... Yes.... Well, thanks.... Sue says thank you, too.... Bye. *(He hangs up. To Susan)* There you go. Sorted!

SUSAN Sorted!?

ANDREW Yes.

SUSAN Your dad put his little finger in Samuel and Eleanor's dinner three times and you say 'sorted'!?

ANDREW I'm sure he washed his hands before he did it.

SUSAN Are you? I'm not.

ANDREW Oh, come on now, Sue.

SUSAN	And you do remember when we saw him at Christmas that he showed us that fungal infection on his little finger!
ANDREW	That's cleared up now. Anyway; he does have another little finger.
SUSAN	Which is usually covered in engine oil, or something else, which that disgusting old car of his chooses to leak on a weekly basis.
ANDREW	*(trying to calm the situation)* Look, it's done now. I'm sure they'll be fine, Sue.
SUSAN	We'll have to wait and see, won't we? Let's just hope that Samuel and Eleanor don't come down with salmonella!
ANDREW	Salmonella! Oh, really, Sue.
SUSAN	And please stop calling me Sue. I'm Susan. I always have been and I always will be!
ANDREW	*(continuing to try and keep things calm)* I'm sorry, Susan, I'm sorry. It's just easier to say Sue. That's all.
SUSAN	You always shorten names, don't you?
ANDREW	I don't go out of my way to do it. It just happens naturally.
SUSAN	You shorten my name. You shorten the children's names.
ANDREW	I know. I'm sorry. I didn't know you were that bothered by it.
SUSAN	All your previous girlfriend's names were shortened.
ANDREW	What!?
SUSAN	All the women you had... *(searching for the correct word)* relations with, before you met me, had their names shortened.

ANDREW   Sorry. I'm not sure what this has got…

SUSAN   Bernadette was Bernie. Elizabeth was Lizzie.

ANDREW   My God! How do you remember all these things?

SUSAN   Christine was Chris…and, and…

ANDREW   And Anne was Anne and Kate was Kate!

SUSAN   Ok, ok, smart arse, you know what I mean!

ANDREW   No, Susan, I really don't know what you mean.

SUSAN   I'm your wife!

ANDREW   And?

SUSAN   And I want to be different to them!

ANDREW   You are different. *(Raising his voice)* You're the one I married!

SUSAN   *(slightly taken aback)* Yes, well, there's no need to shout.

ANDREW   *(quieter)* You're the one I love.

SUSAN   Yes…I know…I'm sorry.

ANDREW   *(calming down)* No; I'm sorry. I just can't follow the thread and *(holding Susan)* whatever your name is; I married you. I didn't marry any of those others; I married you. And I didn't marry you because you're Susan or Sue, but because you're you. *(Pause)* Anyway, Susan, let's get back to your assumption that the presence of my dad's little finger in Samuel and Eleanor's dinner will have given them salmonella!

SUSAN   It might have.

ANDREW   There's no way that Sam 'n' Ella could have caught salmonella fr-

19

SUSAN	*(fuming and heading into the bathroom)* You just had to shorten their names one more time. Didn't you?
ANDREW	*(holding his hands up)* Completely unintentional. Sorry.

Long pause

ANDREW	*(calling)* They'll be ok.
SUSAN	*(calling back)* I know.
ANDREW	*(checking his watch)* We're going to miss dinner if we don't hurry up.
SUSAN	I'm not very hungry any more.
ANDREW	Oh.
SUSAN	*(popping her head round the door)* How about you?
ANDREW	Well, I suppose I haven't got much of an appetite.
SUSAN	No?
ANDREW	No.
SUSAN	I think I'll run that bath, then. *(She returns to the bathroom)*
ANDREW	*(calling after her)* Ok. I'll just sit here and…relax, I guess. *(He sits on the bed, leaning on the headboard)*

Sound of running water off. Andrew sits for a while, but clearly can't relax. He gets up and peers out of the window, then he sits on each seat in the room before he eventually goes into his bag and removes a copy of The Times newspaper and a pen and returns to the bed

ANDREW	*(to himself)* Right, Times crossword. You're mine. *(He folds the paper accordingly, and settles down)* One across… *(he mumbles the clue to himself and starts thinking; sucking the end of his pen etc)* Ok, I'll come back to you. One down… *(more mumbling)* Ah, yes, now then you're…. you're…. going to wait over there with one across! Two across…

Bath water stops running

SUSAN *(calling)* You alright in there?

ANDREW *(calling)* Yes. How's the bath?

SUSAN Very nice. What are you doing?

ANDREW Oh, er, just The Times crossword.

SUSAN Really? I didn't know you did that.

ANDREW *(he is writing in letters and crossing them out again)* Oh, you know, on occasion.

SUSAN How's this one going?

ANDREW *(more crossing out)* Oh, not too bad. Only just started really.

Andrew's phone 'pings.' He's received an email or text message. He reaches for his phone

SUSAN Was that your phone?

ANDREW *(looking at his phone)* Yes. *(Under his breath)* Damn.

SUSAN I thought you'd turned it off.

ANDREW Yes. I meant to.

SUSAN You said you would after George's third email.

ANDREW *(typing a reply)* It's not from George. It's just spam. I'm turning it off now.

SUSAN I know he's your boss, but you don't have to reply to him when you're on holiday.

ANDREW *(still typing his reply)* I know. Phone's off now.

SUSAN Good.

Andrew continues to type some more and eventually turns his phone off and puts it away

ANDREW	Nice bath?
SUSAN	Yes, thank you. It's helping to relax me.
ANDREW	Good.
SUSAN	Sorry about earlier. You know. All my blurting out and having a go at you for shortening names and things.
ANDREW	That's ok. I'm sorry if I upset you at all.
SUSAN	That's fine. *(Pause)* Have you finished that crossword yet?
ANDREW	*(looking at the paper he's cast aside)* Erm, not yet. Why?
SUSAN	I'm just about to get out of the bath.
ANDREW	Really? That was a bit quick!
SUSAN	I know. I was just wondering if you'd like to try working on the romance I mentioned earlier?
ANDREW	*(has been fiddling with his pen and flicks the top off at the thought of romance and fumbles through the bed clothes looking for it)* Oh, er, right. Yes… please!
SUSAN	*(laughing)* I'll get ready in here, whilst you hop into bed and wait for me.
ANDREW	Oh, right.

Andrew starts to get undressed in a slightly excited fashion. Taking a sock off and falling onto the bed, etc.

SUSAN	*(calling from the bathroom)* You alright?
ANDREW	Yes, just having trouble with a sock, that's all!
SUSAN	You can have trouble with me in a few minutes!
ANDREW	*(laughing whilst wrestling with his shirt buttons)* Lovely!

Andrew continues to undress, turns on the bedside lamp and gets into bed in his underwear. Pause

ANDREW You alright in there?

SUSAN Yes. Just having difficulty with flushing the toilet.

ANDREW Oh, well, just leave it for now.

SUSAN I'd rather not.

ANDREW Why not?

SUSAN Well, it's a number two and I'd rather not just leave it floating there.

ANDREW *(to himself)* And who says romance is dead!

SUSAN What's that?

ANDREW Nothing. Do you want a hand?

SUSAN No. I think I've got it now; I'll be in soon.

ANDREW Right.

Andrew sits in bed and waits. He sniffs his armpits and decides they could smell better. He gets deodorant from his bag and sprays a bit under each arm and liberally sprays under the duvet cover. He places the deodorant on the bedside table and picks up the Bible which is sat on there

ANDREW Blimey. A Bible in a double room. Let's hope it doesn't come to that!

He replaces the Bible as Susan enters wearing a very unflattering long flannelette nightie

ANDREW Oh!

SUSAN Alright?

ANDREW Yes. I just thought you'd be wearing something, well, a little more sexy.

SUSAN *(looking down at herself)* Oh, God. Do you know, I didn't think about it.

ANDREW Oh, right.

SUSAN I just intended to put something nice on and then between the number two and the trouble with flushing the loo, I must have forgotten what I'd planned to put on.

ANDREW Right.

SUSAN Sorry.

ANDREW That's ok. *(Pointing at the nightie)* I'm just not quite sure why you put that thing in your bag in the first place.

SUSAN I don't know, really. Habit, I guess.

ANDREW Habit?

SUSAN Well, I do wear it a lot at home.

ANDREW True.

SUSAN *(feeling the material)* And the children like the feel of it.

ANDREW Right.

SUSAN *(trying to be sexy)* You might like the feel of it, too!

ANDREW Might I?

SUSAN *(approaching the bed)* Do you want to feel it; or shall I make you wait longer by going to get changed?

ANDREW I think I'd like to feel it.

SUSAN Right!

Susan quickly hops into bed. They disappear under the duvet

SUSAN *(from under the duvet)* Does it feel nice?

ANDREW (under the duvet) Oh, yes!

SUSAN (under the duvet) Mmmm....

ANDREW (under the duvet) Hang on!

SUSAN (under the duvet) What?

ANDREW (under the duvet) What's that (coming out from under the duvet and taking a big gasp of air) smell!?

SUSAN (also coming out from under the duvet) What smell?

ANDREW A not very pleasant smell. I'm sure I recognise it.

SUSAN Where?

ANDREW On your nightie somewhere, I think.

SUSAN Really?

ANDREW (pointing at one of Susan's shoulders) I think I was around there when I smelled it.

SUSAN (pointing at a shoulder) Here?

ANDREW Yes.

SUSAN (sniffing it) Oh, that's just a bit of sick.

ANDREW Sick!?

SUSAN Well; just the smell of sick.

ANDREW Oh, just the smell of sick.

SUSAN As in, I removed the sick, but the smell remains.

ANDREW Yes, I know the smell remains!

SUSAN (still sniffing) It's not too bad.

ANDREW Maybe not. But it's not particularly romantic, is it?

SUSAN No. I suppose not.

ANDREW I would've thought that you'd have only packed that thing if it was clean.

SUSAN It was clean, until Eleanor was sick on it after lunch.

ANDREW Right.

Pause

SUSAN Do you want to carry on?

ANDREW I don't think my nose will allow me to.

SUSAN *(smiling)* Would your nose like me to change?

ANDREW *(returning the smile)* Yes, please!

SUSAN *(kissing him on the nose)* Wait there.

Susan exits to the bathroom. Andrew sniffs the air and picks up his can of deodorant and sprays into the air and under the duvet

ANDREW *(calling)* You ok?

SUSAN *(from the bathroom)* Yes, just having trouble with the loo handle again.

ANDREW Again?

SUSAN Yes.

ANDREW Not another number two, surely!?

SUSAN No, no. Just a quick number one.

ANDREW Leave it then.

SUSAN No, it's ok. There's a knack to it. Once I've got it I can show you how to do it!

ANDREW *(not very enthusiastically)* Great!

SUSAN Won't be long.

ANDREW Ok.

Andrew looks around and decides to read his can of deodorant which he is still holding

ANDREW *(reading from the deodorant)* The best for men. *(Sniffing the air)* Pretty good for sick, too!

He replaces the can and picks up the Bible. He thumbs through to Genesis 1

ANDREW *(reading)* 'In the beginning, God created the heavens and the earth.' I suppose that's as good a place to start as any. *(Reading)* 'The earth was without form and void, and darkness was over the face of the deep' some parts haven't changed much! 'And the Spirit of God was hovering over the face of the waters.' *(Shivering)* Spooky! 'And God said, "Let there be light,"* (Susan re-enters from the bathroom wearing a more appropriate, shorter, nightie/negligee. Andrew looks up, closes the Bible and returns it to his bedside table)* and there was light!'

SUSAN Is this a little better?

ANDREW Much.

SUSAN *(approaching the bed)* Good!

ANDREW *(smiling)* As long as it's clean!

SUSAN *(smiling)* It's clean. You can smell it for yourself. *(She gets into bed)*

ANDREW Ok!

They disappear under the duvet once more. Lots of rolling around and giggling etc

SUSAN *(shouting suddenly)* Marmite!

ANDREW *(reacting by swiftly lifting his head up, but remaining under the duvet)* What?!

SUSAN *(even louder)* Marmite!!

ANDREW *(appearing out of the top of the duvet)* Oh, right! Marmite. *(He jumps out of bed and starts pacing around. Muttering to himself)* Marmite, Marmite. In my bag. *(He looks in his bag)* No, not in my bag. Ah! Wash bag! In the bathroom. *(He heads towards the bathroom and stops. To himself)* Marmite!? Why does she want Marmite? We've never used Marmite before. Now, chocolate spread. She probably means chocolate spread. I've probably got her so excited that she's just got her 'preserves' muddled up! Now, I know I've got some chocolate spread in my wash bag. *(He exits to the bathroom)*

SUSAN *(appearing above the duvet. Calling)* Andrew!

ANDREW *(from the bathroom)* Yes.

SUSAN What are you doing?

ANDREW Just getting what you requested.

SUSAN Pardon?

ANDREW *(re-entering from the bathroom)* Just getting this! *(He holds up a jar of chocolate spread)*

SUSAN What's that?

ANDREW What you asked for. Well, what I assumed you meant to ask for!

SUSAN That's chocolate spread.

ANDREW Yes, I know.

SUSAN What are you doing with chocolate spread in the bathroom?

ANDREW It was in my wash bag.

SUSAN Ok. What are you doing with chocolate spread in your wash bag?

ANDREW I put it in there. Just in case.

SUSAN	Just in case what?
ANDREW	Just in case you wanted it. Which you do.
SUSAN	Do I?
ANDREW	Well, you did just shout it out.
SUSAN	No I didn't. I shouted out Marmite.
ANDREW	Well, yes, I know you shouted out Marmite, but I assumed you meant chocolate spread seeing as we've never used Marmite before and I can't stand the stuff!
SUSAN	Oh, I see.
ANDREW	So?
SUSAN	I thought I'd packed the chocolate spread in with the children's stuff.
ANDREW	Oh, you did. This is a brand-new jar I got just for us!
SUSAN	Aaah. You went and bought a new jar, just for us. How sweet!
ANDREW	*(starting to open the jar)* Shall we?
SUSAN	Hang on.
ANDREW	What?
SUSAN	That's not what I meant.
ANDREW	Oh, wasn't it?
SUSAN	No.
ANDREW	What did you mean?
SUSAN	I meant what I said; Marmite.
ANDREW	But I can't stand the stuff and it's all sort of gloopy and…

SUSAN No, not for anything naughty; but for the children.

ANDREW The what?

SUSAN The children. I said it because I suddenly remembered that I forgot to pack the Marmite for the children.

ANDREW *(replacing the lid on the jar of chocolate spread)* So, it wasn't anything at all to do with us, under the duvet. It was another of your blurted-out words.

SUSAN Yes.

ANDREW I suppose I should put this back then?

SUSAN Yes.

Andrew trudges off to the bathroom and returns without the jar

ANDREW *(deflated)* What do you want to do now?

SUSAN Phone your mum, again.

ANDREW Really?

SUSAN Yes.

ANDREW And say what?

SUSAN That I forgot to pack the Marmite.

ANDREW But, you did pack the chocolate spread.

SUSAN Yes.

ANDREW So, the children can have that on their toast for breakfast.

SUSAN But, I usually give them a choice.

ANDREW I know you do. But I'm sure they'll cope if my mum just says 'oh, look, it's chocolate spread on toast, today', and gives it to them.

SUSAN Maybe.

ANDREW *(getting back into bed)* They'll be fine. Trust me.

SUSAN Ok. Sorry.

ANDREW *(starting to snuggle up)* Now then; where were we…?

SUSAN I don't think I'm up for anything, now.

ANDREW Oh.

SUSAN I think I'm too tired.

ANDREW Right.

SUSAN It's been quite a stressful day, with one thing and another. I thought the bath had relaxed me, but it clearly hasn't.

ANDREW No.

SUSAN Sorry. You don't mind, do you?

ANDREW *(clearly disgruntled)* No, no….

SUSAN Good. *(Kissing him on his cheek)* Night, night, then.

ANDREW Night.

They both start to snuggle down

SUSAN Can you close the curtains, please.

ANDREW *(getting back out of bed)* Oh, right.

Andrew closes the curtains, gets back into bed and turns off the bedside lamp.

Pause

ANDREW Blimey. It's dark.

SUSAN What's that?

ANDREW I said it's dark.

SUSAN   Yes.

ANDREW   Much darker than at home.

SUSAN   Well, we're in the countryside aren't we. Much darker in the countryside than at home.

ANDREW   I suppose so.

SUSAN   No light pollution out here.

ANDREW   True. But you'd have thought they'd have had some lights on the car park.

SUSAN   Mmmm.

ANDREW   A bit of light seeping round the edge of the curtains.

SUSAN   Mmmm.

ANDREW   I'm used to that bit of light. *(Pause)* Don't like it this dark. *(Pause)* Have you got one of those plug-in lights, like we've got on the landing at home?

SUSAN   No. The children have it at your parents.

ANDREW   Oh. *(Pause)* I don't think I can sleep with it being this dark.

SUSAN   Just close your eyes.

ANDREW   But what happens when I open them?

SUSAN   *(getting annoyed)* What?

ANDREW   Well, when I wake up in the night and open my eyes and it's this dark, I won't know whether I've actually opened them or not.

SUSAN   What?

ANDREW   I like to have a clear difference when my eyes are open or closed, so I know what state I'm in.

SUSAN   I have no idea what state you're in.

ANDREW	What?
SUSAN	Just open the curtains a bit.
ANDREW	*(giving it some thought)* I could, but in the morning it'll probably be too bright. Plus, we might find someone in the car park peering in!
SUSAN	No one will be peering in, we're on the second floor!
ANDREW	Oh, you know what I mean.
SUSAN	*(turning over with her back towards Andrew)* I'm sorry, Andrew, I don't know what to suggest. I just need some sleep.
ANDREW	Ok. *(Pause)* I think I'll put the bathroom light on and leave the door slightly ajar. *(No response from Susan. Getting out of bed)* I'll do that and have a wee while I'm in there. *(He exits to the bathroom)*

Pause

ANDREW	*(in a raised whisper from the bathroom)* I can't flush the loo. Susan. You never showed me how to flush the loo. *(Re-entering from the bathroom)* Susan! *(Pause)* Great. I wish I could go to sleep like that!

Andrew gets back into bed. He tosses and turns for a while and eventually sits up in bed and turns the bedside lamp on. He looks at Susan. Looks around the room for a bit and finally picks up the Bible

ANDREW	*(thumbing through the Bible)* Right. We've done the start. Let's try somewhere random…. *(opening and reading from the Bible)* Luke 9: 'And he said unto them, "Take nothing for your journey, no staff, nor bag, nor money" – *(laughing to himself)* nor night light – "and do not have two tunics." I can confirm that I do not have two tunics! *(He chuckles again)* "And from whatever house you enter, stay there, and from there depart."' I suppose if you didn't depart, you'd stay there forever. Mmmm…. *(turning the page)* 'But he said to them, "You give them something to eat." – I could do with something to eat – They said "We have no more than five loaves and two fish"' – that's more than I've

had. I wonder if they had Marmite or chocolate spread?

Andrew continues to chuckle as he flicks through the Bible. He picks up his pen and starts to make notes in the margin as lights fade to black out

Scene 2

Next morning, Friday. Susan and Andrew have left and the room is a bit dishevelled with the duvet strewn across the bed, etc. A moment, then two chambermaids enter. Megan carries clean bed linen and Trish carries a small plastic holder with cleaning fluids and cloths for the bathroom. Both are 40+ and like a good gossip about the hotel guests.

MEGAN *(mid-sentence)* .... I don't know how you got that off, Trish.

TRISH Usual way, Megan, lots of elbow grease.

MEGAN But it looked decidedly worse than other ones we've had.

TRISH It was.

MEGAN What do you think it was?

They start to change the bed linen under the following

TRISH Not 100% sure. But if I had to hazard a guess, I'd say a mistimed bath bomb.

MEGAN Oh. Why mistimed?

TRISH Well; normally a bath bomb which has been put in early doors, when you're supposed to put it in, when the hot tap is still running, dissipates evenly through the bath water. Leaving the fizz, but only leaving a minor residue tide mark which is easily wiped off with your average J-cloth.

MEGAN Right.

TRISH Whereas, the mistimed bomb, which is often put in too late, doesn't dissolve fully, leaving clumps floating around the bath.

MEGAN Nice.

TRISH And then, the bath isn't emptied straight afterwards, but left until the following morning before the plug is removed.

MEGAN I see.

TRISH Put that all together with the passion fruit flavour, which I could distinctly smell in room 25, and you've got a recipe for a killer tide mark!

MEGAN Oh, you are good, Trish.

TRISH Thank you.

MEGAN I love watching you work. Such an artist.

TRISH *(picking up her cleaning stuff)* You alright finishing in here, Megan, while I go and see what delights are to be found in this bathroom? *(She exits to the bathroom)*

MEGAN Sure. *(Raising her voice so Trish can hear her from the bathroom)* Funny couple.

TRISH *(calling back)* Who are?

MEGAN The ones in this room, last night.

TRISH Were they?

MEGAN Yes.

TRISH Why's that?

MEGAN Gary was waiting tables last night and he got asked not once, but twice whether the food was freshly cooked or whether it was frozen and warmed up in a microwave.

TRISH Really?

MEGAN Yes.

TRISH Then what happened?

MEGAN Gary went and told Chef.

TRISH   Oh, dear.

MEGAN   Chef went potty and told all the waiters and waitresses to find out who'd been spreading the rumour.

TRISH   Right.

MEGAN   The result was that the two couples who made the enquiry had both shared the lift with a couple who had joined them from the second floor and this couple had booked for dinner and then never turned up!

TRISH   *(finding it all too exciting, she returns from the bathroom)* So, what happened next?

MEGAN   Chef decided to come up to this room after his shift last night to try and find out if it was this couple.

TRISH   And?

MEGAN   He was about to knock on the door when he heard voices.

TRISH   Voices? Coming from where?

MEGAN   From in here.

TRISH   What; were they arguing?

MEGAN   No. He actually said the voices were quite quiet and he realised that the man was talking to himself!

TRISH   To himself?

MEGAN   Yes. And what's more, he was putting lots of different accents on!

TRISH   What?!

MEGAN   Chef says he listened for a few minutes and worked out that he was reading from the Bible.

TRISH   Really?

MEGAN And that he was putting on a different voice for each person!

TRISH Well I never!

MEGAN He said he heard Jesus and the 12 Disciples all with different accents! He said there was a posh Peter, an Australian Andrew, a Jamaican Judas and a Geordie Jesus!

TRISH *(laughing)* Brilliant! Then what happened?

MEGAN Well, Chef decided to leave it.

TRISH I bet he did.

MEGAN All a bit freaky. Even for him!

TRISH *(returning to the bathroom)* I'll have to have a word with Chef later. See if he can remember all the different accents.

MEGAN *(laughing)* Yes.

Pause

TRISH *(calling from the bathroom)* So, they didn't take their meal in the restaurant, then?

MEGAN No, apparently not.

TRISH I think I know why. *(Returning from the bathroom, holding up the jar of chocolate spread)* They ate in here!

MEGAN Where did you find that?

TRISH Under the pile of dirty towels.

MEGAN Really?

TRISH Yep!

MEGAN This job never fails to fascinate me.

TRISH Me too, Megan. Every day is different!

MEGAN *(pointing towards the complimentary tray)* Are the biscuits gone?

TRISH *(looking down at the small, sealed pack of biscuits)* No, why?

MEGAN Well, I thought they might have dipped the shortbread into it.

TRISH I doubt it was the shortbread that was being dipped into it!

MEGAN What... you don't mean?

TRISH I do!

MEGAN Open it and have a look.

TRISH I don't want to open it and have a look.

MEGAN Go on.

TRISH No. If you want to have a look, you open it.

MEGAN *(making her way to Trish and taking the jar)* Come here. *(Opening it)* Sealed!

TRISH What?

MEGAN *(showing her)* Look. The inner seal is still intact.

TRISH So, nothing was dipped in it.

MEGAN *(replacing the lid)* Apparently not.

TRISH So; no dinner and no chocolate spread.

MEGAN Any tide mark around the bath?

TRISH A faint one. It looks like a quick shallow bath for one is all that was taken.

MEGAN How do you know it was only a bath for one?

TRISH Experience, Megan. However little the volume of water which was put in that bath, the presence of two people would have brought that tide mark up considerably higher than the faint one left in there.

MEGAN Oh, I see.

TRISH Simple science, Megan.

MEGAN I see. What a shame…

They gather up all the dirty washing and all their other bits and head towards the door

TRISH Well; if I'd had a night like that, I'd have probably ended up reading the Bible and started giving all the disciples accents.

MEGAN *(as they exit)* Me too!

Lights fade to black out

Scene 3

The same. The room is neat and tidy, as the maids left it. 6pm. George and Caroline enter. Both are in their 60's. Caroline is a little forgetful. George is a grumpy man who runs his own large, successful business and is used to getting his own way. George enters first.

GEORGE   Ah, here we are, number 27.

CAROLINE   *(carrying two small cases and placing them on the floor)* Yes.

GEORGE   *(looking around)* It's a bit plain.

CAROLINE   What is?

GEORGE   The room.

CAROLINE   Is it?

GEORGE   Yes. Don't you think?

CAROLINE   *(looking around)* It's ok.

GEORGE   Ok! Ok? That's like calling something 'nice.'

CAROLINE   Yes, it is.

GEORGE   What is?

CAROLINE   The room.

GEORGE   What about it?

CAROLINE   It's nice.

GEORGE   Good grief.

CAROLINE   What's that, George?

GEORGE   Nothing, Caroline. *(Pause)* Who recommended this place to you?

CAROLINE   Oh, I can't remember. Somebody.

GEORGE   Yes, well, I suppose it must have been somebody.

CAROLINE   Yes, it was.

GEORGE   Good grief. Your memory's getting worse, isn't it?

CAROLINE   My memory? It's not that bad.

GEORGE   Not that bad! Ok, what did you have for breakfast?

CAROLINE   When?

GEORGE   This morning. At approximately breakfast time.

CAROLINE   This morning?

GEORGE   Yes, this morning.

CAROLINE   For breakfast?

GEORGE   Yes. For breakfast. This morning.

CAROLINE   Right, well, it was either toast or porridge.

GEORGE   Ok, and which one are you going to plump for?

CAROLINE   Mmmm?

GEORGE   Which one? Toast or porridge?

CAROLINE   Erm… *(taking her time)* … toast.

GEORGE   No.

CAROLINE   No?

GEORGE   No.

CAROLINE   Oh.

GEORGE   You had grapefruit.

CAROLINE   Did I?

GEORGE   Yes.

CAROLINE How do you know what I had?

GEORGE *(raising his voice a little)* Because I made it for you!

CAROLINE Did you?

GEORGE Yes. I sliced it in half and even put one of those sticky cherries on the top!

CAROLINE Oh, yes, so you did. Thank you.

GEORGE You're welcome. I thought you'd have remembered, seeing as I don't usually make you breakfast.

CAROLINE That's true.

GEORGE What is?

CAROLINE That you don't usually make me breakfast.

GEORGE Well. It's a holiday, isn't it?

CAROLINE Yes.

GEORGE Yes. One night here; then on to the port tomorrow.

CAROLINE Yes.

GEORGE *(Pause. Looking around the room)* Have we stayed here before?

CAROLINE Sorry?

GEORGE This hotel. Have we stayed here before?

CAROLINE I don't know. I don't think so, why?

GEORGE Just something vaguely familiar.

CAROLINE Well, we've been in so many hotels, they all start to merge in your memory.

GEORGE *(muttering)* Everything merges in your memory.

CAROLINE Pardon?

GEORGE I said 'possibly.'

CAROLINE I mean; when you've seen one hotel room you've seen them all!

GEORGE I'd normally agree with you on that, Caroline, but not this room. My God. This room's terrible.

CAROLINE *(taking out her make-up bag and sitting at the dressing table)* It's ok.

GEORGE *(raising his eyebrows then looking at the wallpaper)* It's not ok. Have you seen this wallpaper?

CAROLINE *(starting to apply make-up, etc)* What about it?

GEORGE It's ancient.

CAROLINE Is it?

GEORGE Faded browny-yellow.

CAROLINE It's ok.

GEORGE Will you please stop it with the 'ok'. It's not ok. It's terrible.

CAROLINE Sorry, George.

GEORGE Why we went on the recommendation of… 'somebody', rather than use our usual stopover hotel.

CAROLINE You booked it, George. You could have booked the other place.

GEORGE I didn't book it. My secretary did.

CAROLINE Then it's your fault for making Linda do personal things for you. She's your business secretary not your PA.

GEORGE It's not my fault, it's your friend 'somebody's' fault. If Linda didn't want to book it for me, she could have said no.

CAROLINE   People can't say no to you, George, and you know it.

GEORGE   I am the boss.

CAROLINE   Quite! *(Pause)* It's just one night. We'll cope.

GEORGE   Mmm. *(Looking around)* I'm sure you said your 'somebody' said this place was four-star.

CAROLINE   I can't remember.

GEORGE   No, I don't suppose you can.

CAROLINE   Why?

GEORGE   Because the sign outside distinctly said two-star.

CAROLINE   *(continuing with her make-up)* If you'd done the booking, instead of leaving it to Linda, you'd have probably noticed that.

GEORGE   Mmm. I'm guessing your friend 'somebody' came some time ago and this place has just gone to the dogs, like the rest of this country.

CAROLINE   Maybe.

GEORGE   I mean, the state of this wallpaper suggests it's been a long time since a redecoration's taken place.

CAROLINE   If you say so.

GEORGE   It probably lost one star for that.

CAROLINE   Probably.

GEORGE   *(pacing around the room)* I wonder what else drops a hotel from four-star to two-star?

CAROLINE   No idea.

GEORGE   I wonder. *(He places his suitcase on the bed and removes a few items including a pair of smart trousers)* These trousers have got a little creased in the case.

CAROLINE   Oh dear.

GEORGE   *(heading towards the door)* I'll just… What!

CAROLINE   What is it?

GEORGE   I can't believe it.

CAROLINE   What's that?

GEORGE   *(in utter disbelief)* No trouser press!

CAROLINE   *(looking up)* What?

GEORGE   No trouser press!

CAROLINE   Really?

GEORGE   Yes, look!

CAROLINE   Oh, yes. Have you looked anywhere else?

GEORGE   Why would I look anywhere else? They're always behind the door.

CAROLINE   Are they?

GEORGE   Yes! Every hotel, behind the door, trouser press! *(Pointing near to the door)*

CAROLINE   Really?

GEORGE   Yes.

CAROLINE   I'd never noticed.

GEORGE   Well, there's a surprise!

Pause

CAROLINE   Have you tried the bathroom?

GEORGE   Why on Earth would it be in the bathroom?

CAROLINE   Why not?

GEORGE   Because it's an electrical item. That's why not!

CAROLINE   Oh, yes. Isn't it worth a quick check in there?

GEORGE   I suppose so. *(Heading towards the bathroom)* Looking at the state of this place it probably does store its electrical devices near the water source! *(He exits to the bathroom)*

CAROLINE   *(returning to her make-up and calling)* Any luck?

GEORGE   *(calling)* No. Good grief!

CAROLINE   What?

GEORGE   The grouting in here's terrible.

CAROLINE   Really?

GEORGE   *(returning)* Yes. Clearly not been replaced for donkey's years either.

CAROLINE   No?

GEORGE   No. Well at least we now know how they lost the two stars.

CAROLINE   Do we?

GEORGE   Oh yes. One star for clearly not redecorating in more than a generation and one for no trouser press.

CAROLINE   Maybe.

GEORGE   Right. *(Heading towards the bed)* I'm going to ring down to reception to complain.

CAROLINE   Ok. But, do remember we're only here for one night.

GEORGE   *(sitting on the bed)* That's by the by, Caroline. *(Realising there's no phone)* What the…. *(he starts to look in/under the bedside table, under the bed and even under the pillow)*

CAROLINE   What is it now?

GEORGE   No bloody phone!

CAROLINE   *(looking up)* Really?

GEORGE   Yes!

CAROLINE   Never mind. Use your mobile.

GEORGE   Use my mobile!?

CAROLINE   Yes.

GEORGE   I'm not going to use my mobile just to phone down to reception. There should be a phone here.

CAROLINE   Well, phone them to tell them.

GEORGE   I can't. There's no phone!

CAROLINE   Use your mobile.

GEORGE   *(putting his head in his hands)* God, give me strength. *(Pause)* Not decorated, no trouser press and no phone. This place should only have one star.

CAROLINE   *(resuming her make-up)* True.

GEORGE   Although I don't think I've ever seen a one-star hotel…

Pause. George sits back on the bed and picks up the Bible

GEORGE   *(holding the Bible)* Look at that.

CAROLINE   *(without looking up)* What's that?

GEORGE   The Bible.

CAROLINE   Oh, right.

GEORGE   No phone. But still a Bible.

CAROLINE   Yes.

George starts to flick through the Bible

CAROLINE *(Pausing from her make-up and looking over at George)* I've often wondered what people from other religions make of that.

GEORGE *(looking up)* What?

CAROLINE The Bible in their hotel room.

GEORGE What do you mean?

CAROLINE Well, I mean, I know we're a predominantly Christian country, but aren't we supposed to be multi-cultural and accepting of all other faiths?

GEORGE Don't start me on that, Caroline.

CAROLINE No. I'm not trying to start you on that, George.

GEORGE I'm on holiday, Caroline. A break from unions and equality and…

CAROLINE *(interjecting)* I know, George, that's why I'm not starting on it. But, knowing all the stuff you have to do at work to come across as being fair…

GEORGE Come across? I don't just come across as being fair. I am fair!

CAROLINE Yes, I'm sure you are. But, my point is, with all the hoops you have to jump through; why only a Bible?

GEORGE *(giving it some thought)* You mean; why isn't there a Qur'an or other religious texts in the room?

CAROLINE Exactly.

GEORGE I don't know. That's a very good point.

CAROLINE Maybe you could ask the hotel.

GEORGE I would if there was a phone…. *(looking back at the Bible and stopping at a certain point in it)* Hello. What's this?

CAROLINE What?

GEORGE *(looking in the Bible)* Someone's been scribbling in the Bible.

CAROLINE Oh, dear. That's not very respectful.

GEORGE In the margin next to some bit about the Disciples.

CAROLINE Oh, yes?

GEORGE It looks like some sort of joke about an Australian, a Jamaican and a Geordie.

CAROLINE Oh; I hope the punchline isn't rude as that would be disrespectful.

GEORGE Yes. I can't seem to see a punchline.

CAROLINE Probably best.

GEORGE Yes.

George closes the Bible and feels the weight of it. He then looks at his creased trousers laying on the bed

GEORGE Have you finished doing your make-up?

CAROLINE Yes, I'm ready for dinner when you are.

GEORGE Right. Can I use that stool a minute?

CAROLINE Of course.

Caroline gets up and George takes the stool and places it centre stage

CAROLINE What are you doing?

GEORGE Hang on. *(He picks his trousers up and lays them neatly on the stool. He then picks up the Bible and places that on the creased area of the trousers)* There!

CAROLINE You can't do that.

GEORGE Why not?

CAROLINE	Well, it's blasphemy, or something, isn't it?
GEORGE	Of course it isn't. Instead of it laying on the table or bed, it's laying on my trousers. That's all.
CAROLINE	Ironing them.
GEORGE	Hopefully, yes!
CAROLINE	I still think it's a little bit disrespectful.
GEORGE	As long as I don't sit on it, or anything, to try and increase the pressure, I don't think it's disrespectful. It's certainly not as disrespectful as writing a 'three men went into the pub' joke in there!
CAROLINE	I suppose not.
GEORGE	Now, if only they had left a Qur'an and other hefty religious texts in here, I could have pressed a much larger area all at the same time!
CAROLINE	*(smiling)* You are terrible at times, do you know that, George?
GEORGE	*(returning the smile)* Yes. I suppose I do know that!

There's a ring/buzz from George's mobile phone

GEORGE	What's that?
CAROLINE	I think it's your mobile phone. You must have a message, or something.
GEORGE	*(retrieving his phone)* Oh, right. *(Looking at the text message)* Yes. Blast!
CAROLINE	What is it?
GEORGE	It's Simon, at the office. Damn new man at Chilvers and McGraw is questioning his account. Second month running.
CAROLINE	Oh, dear. There's not a lot you can do at this time of night, is there?

GEORGE There's not a lot I can do at any time.

CAROLINE What do you mean?

GEORGE Well, he's a jumped-up little so-and-so who thinks he can breeze in and talk to the boss. Me! Well, he can't.

CAROLINE Right.

GEORGE That's why I have middle managers.

CAROLINE Quite.

GEORGE I'll get Andrew to deal with it. He's on the last day of his holiday, so I'll just call him and give him a quick heads-up so he knows what to expect tomorrow morning, if that's ok?

CAROLINE *(sitting on the bed)* Do you have to? He is on holiday and you said you emailed him several times yesterday.

GEORGE Yes, I did.

CAROLINE That's not fair on the man.

GEORGE He didn't have to reply to them.

CAROLINE Of course he did. You own the company and people can't say no to you.

GEORGE *(punching numbers into his phone)* I can't give Andrew preferential treatment. There's no inequality at my place!

CAROLINE Oh, really, George.

GEORGE *(Holding his hand up. Into phone)* Aah, Andrew. It's George. How are you?.... Good, good; had a nice little break, have you?....Oh, a nice country hotel, that sounds lovely; Caroline and I are holed up in a terrible pit claiming to be two-star, on our way to our cruise.... yours was two-star too, was it?.... Sounds much nicer than this one.... Nice view, as well, eh? I'm not sure what our view's like, hang on, *(looking out of the window)* God, no, you win again, ours is of a car park which is currently housing a huge lorry, in fact I think it's a mobile library; that's a turn up for the books.... yes.... I don't know how they work out the star thing anyway; mine hasn't even got a trouser press, did yours?.... No, well, I suppose if you don't need one you don't look for one.... probably a generation thing, yes.... anyway, that upstart from Chilvers and McGraw is giving Simon a bit of gyp again. Would you mind tackling him tomorrow morning.... yes, well, you sorted him out last time.... yes, well, thanks, Andrew.... I'll leave you to the last few hours of your holiday.... yes, thanks, and send our regards to Susan. Bye.

CAROLINE All sorted?

GEORGE Yes. Good man, Andrew. I've got big things planned for him.

CAROLINE Really?

GEORGE Well; I'm not getting any younger and neither of our girls are interested in the business.

CAROLINE Well, it's hardly surprising is it. Toilets and drains and things.

GEORGE You know we're a lot more than that.

CAROLINE Yes, I know you're a lot more than that.

GEORGE Biggest sanitation company in Southern England.

CAROLINE I know.

GEORGE Seventh biggest in Western Europe.

CAROLINE I thought it was sixth.

GEORGE There is a recession on, you know!

CAROLINE Of course.

GEORGE And the biggest supplier of bidets... outside France, naturally.

CAROLINE Naturally.

GEORGE So, whether the girls like it or not, it's big money; which will continue to keep you in cruises for a very long time if I get someone to take over the reins in the not too distant future.

CAROLINE And you think Andrew's the man?

GEORGE Yes, well, as I said; he's a good man.

CAROLINE Yes, he is.

GEORGE Oh, you remember him?

CAROLINE Yes, I do.

GEORGE Well, that makes a change!

CAROLINE I also remember his mother working for you.

GEORGE *(slightly awkwardly)* Do you?

CAROLINE Don't tell me you've forgotten that?

GEORGE Well, no, now you mention it I think I vaguely remember her.

CAROLINE Only vaguely?

GEORGE Yes, well, I'm surprised you remember her at all; seeing as you couldn't even remember what you had for breakfast.

CAROLINE I remember that she was your first secretary.

GEORGE *(slight bluffing)* Erm, yes, I think that was right.

CAROLINE And you had a bit of a thing for her.

GEORGE *(a little embarrassed)* Don't be silly.

CAROLINE You said you liked the power of being an older woman's boss!

GEORGE (*clearing his throat*) No. Surely not. That doesn't sound like me.

CAROLINE (*laughing*) Ha! Doesn't sound like you! (*Pause*) Then she left, quite quickly, after a year or so.

GEORGE Yes. (*Pause*) Better job offer, I think.

CAROLINE I'm not surprised the amount you used to pay.

GEORGE I gave her the going rate.

CAROLINE Yes, well, I'm surprised you've never asked after her.

GEORGE What do you mean?

CAROLINE You know. Asked Andrew how his mother is.

GEORGE Oh, yes, right. I'll do that some time.

CAROLINE Yes, do. (*Pause*) I can even remember Andrew's children's names.

GEORGE Really? I can't.

CAROLINE Well, I think I can. They're named after some disease, or something.

GEORGE I beg your pardon?

CAROLINE Their names, when put together, sound like some disease or illness.

GEORGE What; like chicken and pox?

CAROLINE Yes, sort of.

GEORGE Good grief. Whatever next!

CAROLINE That's going to bug me, now.

GEORGE What is?

CAROLINE Not remembering their names.

GEORGE   I'd have thought you were used to not remembering things.

CAROLINE   Yes, I know. But their names are on the tip of my tongue, I'm sure.

Pause whilst they both think

    Ruben and Bella?

GEORGE   Ruben and Bella?

CAROLINE   Yes, as in Rubella!

GEORGE   Really?

CAROLINE   No, maybe not.

GEORGE   No. *(Pause)* Scarlet Fever?!

CAROLINE   Is Fever a boy's name?

GEORGE   I think anything seems to be accepted as a name these days.

CAROLINE   True.

GEORGE   I mean, look at that boy our Olivia is with; Dallas, isn't it?

CAROLINE   Yes, it is.

GEORGE   I mean, who calls their son 'Dallas'?

CAROLINE   Someone from Texas?

GEORGE   I shouldn't think so.

CAROLINE   No?

GEORGE   No. That's like someone from Bedfordshire calling their son Luton.

CAROLINE   Yes.

GEORGE Doesn't quite work, does it?

CAROLINE No.

GEORGE No. *(Muttering)* Dallas! *(Pause)* Mind you, I wish he'd taken up that apprenticeship I offered him.

CAROLINE Yes.

GEORGE With two daughters uninterested in the business and our only granddaughter studying... what is she studying at university again?

CAROLINE I can't remember.

GEORGE No, well, whatever it is it's not connected to sanitation. Which means getting her long-term boyfriend in at an apprenticeship level might be a way of keeping it in the family; so to speak.

CAROLINE Yes, well, he might change his mind.

GEORGE I'd like to think so. I mean, I know sanitation might be considered to be at the bottom; quite literally! But surely it's above fish and chip shops!

CAROLINE You would have thought so, yes.

GEORGE Yes. Anyway, shall we go and eat?

CAROLINE Yes. *(Picking up her handbag)* I'm sure Andrew's children's names will come to me during the evening.

GEORGE Yes, well, don't expect too much from this restaurant, seeing as it's a two-star establishment, and a pretty poor one at that. *(Holding the door open)*

CAROLINE *(as she exits)* Ok.

GEORGE For all we know, the chef just takes the food out of the freezer and bungs it in the microwave! *(He exits)*

Lights fade to black out

Scene 4

The following morning, Saturday, George is sitting up in bed, with the bedside lamp on, thumbing through the Bible. Caroline is currently asleep, under the duvet.

A moment, then George starts chuckling at something in the Bible

CAROLINE *(starting to stir)* Is that you, George?

GEORGE Of course it's me. Surely you remember who you went to bed with!

CAROLINE Yes, yes. Just wondering why you're laughing at this time in the morning?

GEORGE It's this Bible.

CAROLINE *(starting to sit up)* What about it?

GEORGE It's so funny.

CAROLINE I never had the Bible down as a comedy.

GEORGE Well, no, it isn't. But this copy has lots of notes in it, by that chap who put the joke in it. Do you remember that, from yesterday?

CAROLINE Yes, yes. I remember that.

GEORGE Well, whenever food is mentioned, which it seems is quite a lot in the Bible, he adds references down the side. Usually about Marmite and chocolate spread.

CAROLINE Ugh. Sounds disgusting.

GEORGE Yes, well, I suppose it would be; but it brightens things up a bit.

CAROLINE Really?

GEORGE *(closing the Bible and replacing it on the bedside table)* Well, it certainly puts a new slant on The Last Supper, that's for sure!

CAROLINE Yes, well, I suppose it would.

Pause

GEORGE How are you feeling, after last night's little embarrassment?

CAROLINE Oh, you know. Not too bad. *(Pause)* I remembered Andrew and Susan's children's names, though. Didn't I?

GEORGE Yes, you did.

CAROLINE That surprised you, didn't it? Me, remembering something.

GEORGE Yes, well, I think you surprised everyone, when you remembered it.

CAROLINE Well, I couldn't help shouting it out. I was so amazed I'd remembered something.

GEORGE Yes; but shouting out 'Sam 'n' Ella' half way through your starter didn't go down too well with the staff, did it?

CAROLINE No.

GEORGE Particularly when your starter was Eggs Benedict!

CAROLINE Yes, well, I did apologise and explain the situation.

GEORGE Yes, well, hopefully the huge tip I left specifically for the chef will have prevented him from letting the tyres down on the Lexus.

CAROLINE I'm sure he wouldn't have done that.

GEORGE I'm not so sure. He looked like someone who's let down a few tyres in his time.

CAROLINE Mmmm.

GEORGE *(getting out of bed and looking in his suitcase)* Right, won't be a mo.

CAROLINE   What are you doing?

GEORGE   *(retrieving a spanner from his case and heading to the bathroom)* Just going to sort the flush out on this toilet.

CAROLINE   Oh, really, George?

GEORGE   *(calling from the bathroom)* Yes, really, Caroline.

CAROLINE   But we're leaving this morning. Can't you just leave it for them to sort out?

GEORGE   *(sticking his head back into the room)* Well, I would have, if the toilet was empty. But, seeing as we were unable to flush it last night, it's, well, it's rather full. So, I'd rather sort it, if you don't mind.

CAROLINE   Ok. But, please be careful.

GEORGE   *(waving his spanner as he exits to the bathroom)* Be careful! I've been in sanitation for 40 years, Caroline. I know exactly what I'm doing. Why do you think I always have my trusty spanner with me?

CAROLINE   *(to herself)* I've often wondered that!

GEORGE   *(calling)* What was that?

CAROLINE   *(calling)* I said I'll make you a cup of tea. Do you fancy that?

GEORGE   Oh, yes please.

CAROLINE   *(heading towards the kettle)* Ok.

GEORGE   Are there any of those little shortbread biscuits there?

CAROLINE   Yes. Yes, there are.

GEORGE   Oh, good. I think I'll have some of those with my tea.

CAROLINE   You'll ruin your breakfast.

GEORGE *(returning from the bathroom, with spanner in hand)* Yes, well, I've been thinking about that and I think it might be wise if we skip breakfast. You, know, after last night and all that.

CAROLINE Really?

GEORGE Well. I do think that it might be a bit awkward when they ask what type of eggs we'd like with our full English. You know; fried, scrambled or poached. We might find a lot of shell in ours.

CAROLINE Yes, you might be right.

GEORGE I think it's probably best if we just leave.

CAROLINE Ok.

GEORGE *(returning to the bathroom, calling)* Fix the toilet, cup of tea, a few biscuits and head off to the port. Get there early and have a nice spot of brunch somewhere. How does that sound?

CAROLINE Lovely.

GEORGE Great.

Brief pause as Caroline pours the tea

CAROLINE Tea's ready.

GEORGE Excellent. We don't have any chocolate spread, do we?

CAROLINE Chocolate spread?!

GEORGE Yes. You know. To dip the biscuits in.

CAROLINE No.

GEORGE Oh.

CAROLINE I didn't even know that you liked chocolate spread.

GEORGE I've never tried it.

CAROLINE Oh.

GEORGE Just fancied giving it a go, after reading about it in the Bible.

CAROLINE Oh. I see. *(Pause)* Do you want me to bring your tea in there for you?

GEORGE No, no. Shan't be long. Well, if I could just get some leverage on this bit here… *(Grunting and groaning)*

CAROLINE Would you like some assistance?

GEORGE *(sticking his head round the door)* Would you mind?

CAROLINE Not at all.

GEORGE I just can't get enough purchase on something and I think, in this case, four hands would be better than two.

CAROLINE Ok.

They both exit to the bathroom

GEORGE *(off)* Now hold that.

CAROLINE *(off)* That?

GEORGE Yes, that.

CAROLINE Ok.

GEORGE And hold it as still as you can whilst I move this.

CAROLINE Ok.

GEORGE Right. Brace yourself, Caroline. Here we go.

Some grunting starts to be heard from George, with the occasional 'ow' from Caroline, as if her fingers have been caught. A moment, then there's a quiet knock on the bedroom door. This is not heard over the noises. A second, slightly louder knock, which still isn't heard. A moment, then Megan and Trish quietly walk in carrying their usual things

MEGAN   *(whispering) Hello? (Pause. She tries again, a little louder) Hello?*

Trish takes hold of Megan's arm and points towards the bathroom. They both stop and listen

GEORGE   *(from the bathroom)* No. I don't think that's going to work.

CAROLINE   *(from the bathroom)* No?

GEORGE   No. I think we need to change positions.

From now on, Megan and Trish proceed to pull faces, nudge each other and stifle laughs as they misunderstand what's going on in the bathroom

CAROLINE   Really?

GEORGE   Oh, yes. I think we've got a much greater chance of getting it in there if we change positions.

CAROLINE   Ok. If you say so. I'll go wherever you want me.

GEORGE   Jolly good. Now; get hold of that and we'll try again. Got it?

CAROLINE   Yes.

GEORGE   Right. Brace yourself again, Caroline. Chocks away!

Megan and Trish both mouth 'chocks away' at each other. Grunting starts again, mostly from George

CAROLINE   I think it's working this time.

GEORGE   Yes. So, do I. It's a bit stiff, but it's coming.

CAROLINE   Yes, I think it is.

Pause

GEORGE   Bingo!

Megan and Trish continue to stifle laughs and mouth 'bingo' at each other

CAROLINE   Well done!

Megan and Trish can't hold themselves any longer. They quickly exit whilst trying not to laugh too loud

GEORGE   *(off)* Thank you, and thank you for your help.

CAROLINE   *(off)* Glad I could help. Now we can flush and leave.

George returns, followed by Caroline

GEORGE   Yes. At least we can leave a clean toilet. I would have hated for the staff to have come in here and thought we were dirty!

Caroline hands George his cup of tea and heads towards her bag to start packing. George stands looking out of the window and sips his tea as lights fade to black out

ACT II

Scene 1

The same, a couple of hours later. Caroline and George have left and the room is a little untidy. A moment, then Megan and Trish enter with the clean linen etc.

TRISH I'm gonna strangle Chef later.

MEGAN You and me both.

TRISH Marking in the book that room 27 had checked out early.

MEGAN *(starting to change the bed sheets etc)* You know why, don't you?

TRISH No.

MEGAN 'Coz you had a dig at him last night for not being brave enough to knock on this room door, the night before, when he heard that chap reading from the Bible.

TRISH It was only a joke. Can't he take a joke?

MEGAN It's Chef, you know, so, no; he can't take a joke!

TRISH Oh, well. They didn't hear us. So, no harm done.

MEGAN No chance of hearing us over the racket they were making!

TRISH I know. I'm a bit worried at what I might find in there *(indicating the bathroom)* this morning.

MEGAN Well; it can't be any worse than what you found in number 21 last week.

TRISH Ugh. Don't mention that. I had to go out and buy a new squeegee after that.

MEGAN I know.

TRISH And management are refusing to pay me back for it.

MEGAN	Are they?
TRISH	Yes.
MEGAN	Why's that?
TRISH	They said I've gone beyond my squeegee allowance for this financial year.
MEGAN	No.
TRISH	Yes.
MEGAN	So, what are you doing about it?
TRISH	I've told them that I only use the squeegee when necessary and that the quality of clientele at this hotel means that its use is required more than it used to be.
MEGAN	What did they say to that?
TRISH	Not a lot. If my squeegee money isn't in my next pay packet, I'm going to the union.
MEGAN	Quite right.

Pause as they continue to change the bed clothes

TRISH	Alright if I make a start on the bathroom?
MEGAN	Go right ahead, Trish.
TRISH	*(picking up her stuff and heading for the bathroom)* Here we go. Wish me luck.
MEGAN	Good luck!

Trish exits to the bathroom whilst Megan finishes off the bed. Pause

TRISH	*(returning from the bathroom holding a spanner)* Looks like they were having even more fun than we thought, Megan!
MEGAN	Blimey! No wonder they couldn't hear us!

TRISH	Well, you know what they say, Megan....
MEGAN	What's that?
TRISH	There's nowt as queer as folk!
MEGAN	True.
TRISH	*(looking at the spanner)* It certainly puts new meaning into the phrase 'spanner in the works'!
MEGAN	*(laughing)* Yes, it does!
TRISH	Right. You ready?
MEGAN	I am; but you haven't done the bathroom, have you?
TRISH	Nothing to do.
MEGAN	Really?
TRISH	Yes. You often find that people who get up to what they were getting up to usually go over the top and leave the bathroom spotless. That's what they've done.
MEGAN	Oh, right.
TRISH	Is this room booked again, for tonight?
MEGAN	A Mr and Mrs Smith.
TRISH	*(exiting the room)* Smith, eh? They'll be unmarried, then.
MEGAN	*(exiting the room)* Probably!

Lights fade to black out

Scene 2

The same. Later the same day in the freshly made-up room. Olivia enters, followed by Dallas. Both are aged around 20, wearing casual clothes of jeans and t-shirts/jumpers etc. Olivia is carrying a small holdall and Dallas has a rucksack on his back.

OLIVIA *(placing her bag on the floor)* This is nice.

DALLAS Yeah, not bad.

OLIVIA Our first night away together and it's in a two-star hotel.

DALLAS *(placing his rucksack on the bed and giving Olivia a hug)* Nothing but the best for my Olivia.

OLIVIA *(returning the hug)* You know that I'd have been more than happy with one-star.

DALLAS I know, and to be honest I was looking for a one-star hotel. But, when I couldn't find any, I found this two-star hotel at the same price as lots of hotels that didn't have any stars. So, I thought it was a great deal!

OLIVIA It's lovely!

DALLAS *(separating from the hug and pointing to the bathroom)* En-suite through there. Kettle there. Sorted!

OLIVIA *(sitting on the bed)* It's great. *(Pause)* Why did you book us in as Mr and Mrs Smith?

DALLAS Well, I mean, it seemed to be the right thing to do, when you're booking a double room. You know, make it sound like you're married.

OLIVIA That's really lovely of you, Dallas, but it's the 21st century and I doubt that hotels have a problem with unmarried couples sharing double rooms, these days.

DALLAS Really?

OLIVIA Really.

DALLAS	Oh. I just didn't want people to look down on us if they thought we were sharing a room before we're married.
OLIVIA	Is that a proposal?
DALLAS	*(slightly wrong footed)* Eh?
OLIVIA	You said 'before we're married'. Suggesting we *are* going to get married.
DALLAS	Did I?
OLIVIA	Yes.
DALLAS	Oh. Erm. Well….
OLIVIA	*(holding his arm)* I'm only teasing. I know what you meant.
DALLAS	Right. Good. I… yes.
OLIVIA	So; why are we Mr and Mrs Smith?
DALLAS	Well, when I phoned up to book, it was the first name that came to me.
OLIVIA	What; even before your own name?
DALLAS	*(laughing)* No. Of course not.
OLIVIA	You could have used your own. I wouldn't have minded.
DALLAS	Well, yes, I suppose I could. But I didn't want to presume.
OLIVIA	*(smiling)* Ok.
DALLAS	You know.
OLIVIA	I know.
DALLAS	Good.

OLIVIA	It's really lovely of you. But you do realise that if you give your name as Mr and Mrs Smith, that the hotel will know that you're unmarried.
DALLAS	Really?
OLIVIA	Oh, yes. Mr and Mrs Smith means unmarried.
DALLAS	Really?
OLIVIA	Yes.
DALLAS	But, what about all the Mr and Mrs Smiths that are married which stay in hotels?
OLIVIA	They pay by card!
DALLAS	What?
OLIVIA	You've got all that cash in your wallet, because you can't pay by card, because you have a different surname written on your card.
DALLAS	True.
OLIVIA	So, even though they might think we're married; as soon as you give them cash they will realise that we're probably not.
DALLAS	*(slightly confused)* So, I should have given my real name, then?
OLIVIA	Well, I wouldn't have minded and you wouldn't have to carry all that cash around with you!
DALLAS	You're too clever for me, Olivia.
OLIVIA	Don't be silly.
DALLAS	You just work things out, which I can't see.
OLIVIA	You booked all this without my help.
DALLAS	Yes. But you'd have done it better.

OLIVIA I'd have done it different. Not better.

Pause

DALLAS I don't know why you put up with me.

OLIVIA What do you mean?

DALLAS You at university. Me still at home.

OLIVIA *(taking his hand)* Because I love you.

DALLAS And I love you, too.

OLIVIA Then that's all we need.

DALLAS Is it?

OLIVIA It's the foundation to build everything else on, isn't it?

DALLAS I guess so. But, after the foundation, what comes next?

OLIVIA Whatever you want, I guess. We're the architects of our future, so I guess we can build on our own foundations any way we want!

DALLAS You, see. You are cleverer than me.

OLIVIA Why do you say that?

DALLAS Because I'd never have been able to come up with all that foundations and architect stuff.

OLIVIA Maybe not, but I'm sure you'd have come up with your own way of describing it.

DALLAS Maybe. But yours would have been better.

OLIVIA Different. Not better!

DALLAS *(smiling)* So, if we are the architects of our own future; what would you build on our foundation of love?!

OLIVIA *(laughing)* Well. I would finish university; start my career and settle down with you. If you'd still want me by then?

DALLAS *(smiling)* Of course I'd still want you. But would you still want me?

OLIVIA Of course. Why wouldn't I?

DALLAS Because you've got university at the moment and a career planned out. I've just got the chip shop.

OLIVIA But, it's a job and you like it. What's the problem?

DALLAS The smell!

OLIVIA Well, yes, apart from that!

DALLAS Can you really see yourself spending your life coming home to a chap who works in a chip shop?

OLIVIA Do you really see yourself working in that chip shop your whole life?

DALLAS I don't know. *(Pause)* You can see your future laid out before you. I can't see beyond the next shift.

OLIVIA You could always take up Grandpa George's offer of an apprenticeship at his place.

DALLAS I know. I'm not sure that sanitation is my thing, though.

OLIVIA I'm not sure that sanitation is anyone's thing. But the experience could help you in lots of ways.

DALLAS How do you mean?

OLIVIA Well, you could learn management skills and then use them to, I don't know, run your own chip shop!

DALLAS *(sounding interested)* Yes. That's a thought.

OLIVIA There are lots of different routes. Maybe we should talk to Grandpa again?

DALLAS   Yes, maybe, but your Grandpa's apprentice wage is less than my chip shop wage. That's why I turned him down in the first place.

OLIVIA   I know. But, it's not all about money.

DALLAS   It is when I'm trying to save for our future together.

OLIVIA   *(taking his hand, once more)* You are so lovely! There's plenty of time for that. I just think you might need to be prepared to slip down the ladder a bit, on the pay front, so you can climb up higher in the future.

DALLAS   See! So much cleverer than me.

OLIVIA   Not at all.

DALLAS   But, what if I don't like it?

OLIVIA   Don't like what?

DALLAS   The apprenticeship.

OLIVIA   Then you find something you do like.

DALLAS   But, that could just be back in a chip shop.

OLIVIA   It doesn't matter. I'll still love you, whatever job you do.

They hug

DALLAS   I don't deserve you.

They separate

OLIVIA   No; I don't deserve you. *(Pause)* Cup of tea?

DALLAS   *(heading to the kettle)* Yes. I'll fill the kettle.

OLIVIA   Thanks.

Dallas heads into the bathroom with the kettle whilst Olivia takes some clothes from her bag and places them in the bedside drawers. Dallas returns with the kettle, replaces it and switches it on

DALLAS There you go. *(Exiting to the bathroom)* Just going to the loo.

OLIVIA *(calling)* What's it like in there?

DALLAS *(calling)* Very nice.

OLIVIA *(calling)* Oh, good.

Pause

Dallas returns from the bathroom holding the toilet handle.

DALLAS *(holding the handle up)* Erm….

OLIVIA *(looking up)* What's that?

DALLAS It's the toilet handle.

OLIVIA Oh. How did you manage that?

DALLAS I just did a wee, went to flush the handle, and it came straight off in my hand!

OLIVIA Oh. Did you flush it too hard; do you think?

DALLAS No. I hardly touched it.

OLIVIA Oh, ok. Have you tried to put it back on?

DALLAS Yes, sort of, but I don't really know where to begin.

OLIVIA No. Nor would I.

DALLAS Oh.

OLIVIA Shame my Grandpa George isn't here. He'd know what to do!

DALLAS Shame I wasn't already his apprentice; then I might know what to do!

They both laugh

OLIVIA *(turning to the bedside table)* Maybe we should call down to reception for assistance. *(Realising there's no phone)* Oh….

DALLAS What?

OLIVIA There isn't a phone.

DALLAS Oh, well, I think I'd probably not wish to tell them anyway.

OLIVIA Why not?

DALLAS You know. Unmarried Mr and Mrs Smith. I think I'd rather not draw any more attention.

OLIVIA Maybe you're right. What do you want to do, then?

DALLAS *(thinking)* Well; *(holding up the toilet handle)* I think I could probably lodge this in the correct place, so the toilet doesn't look broken.

OLIVIA Right.

DALLAS And, then, maybe, we could use the bath!

OLIVIA Use the bath?

DALLAS Yes.

OLIVIA As the toilet?

DALLAS Yes.

OLIVIA I don't think you've thought this through, Dallas.

DALLAS What, no. I see what you mean. I meant just for weeing in.

OLIVIA *(laughing)* Oh, right. I thought you meant for doing everything in!

DALLAS *(laughing)* Oh, no. Ugh!

OLIVIA So, what shall we do about the non-wees?

DALLAS Erm… don't know?

OLIVIA Me neither…

Pause

DALLAS I've just had a thought.

OLIVIA Yes?

DALLAS They must have some toilets downstairs, near the restaurant, mustn't they?

OLIVIA I guess so.

DALLAS We can use them!

OLIVIA When we're down there, maybe. But, what about during the night?

DALLAS Hadn't thought of that.

OLIVIA No.

DALLAS I'll think of something.

OLIVIA Yes.

DALLAS How about you phone your Grandpa?

OLIVIA I can't; he's on a cruise.

DALLAS Oh.

Pause

OLIVIA How about we go and have dinner and think about it down there?

DALLAS Ok.

OLIVIA We might see some toilets nearer than the restaurant.

DALLAS That's a thought.

OLIVIA   Maybe there's one down the corridor, or something?

DALLAS   We can check on the way. Right, are you ready?

OLIVIA   Yes.

DALLAS   Great!

OLIVIA   Oh, just one thing.

DALLAS   What's that?

OLIVIA   How about you have something different to eat tonight.

DALLAS   What do you mean?

OLIVIA   Well, whenever we go out to eat at a restaurant, or suchlike, you always have fish and chips.

DALLAS   I know. I like fish and chips.

OLIVIA   I know you like fish and chips. I like fish and chips, too.

DALLAS   Good. We can both have fish and chips, then.

OLIVIA   We could. But I usually take the opportunity, when at a restaurant, to try different things.

DALLAS   But I might not like the other things.

OLIVIA   True. But you won't know unless you try.

DALLAS   But, if I don't like it, I'd have wasted my money and I'd still be hungry!

OLIVIA   *(taking his arm and heading for the door)* Let's just have a proper look at the menu, before deciding. You never know; they might not even have fish and chips on the menu.

DALLAS   *(exiting)* Oh, don't worry, they have. I checked online before I booked!

They both exit and lights fade to black out

Scene 3

The same, a few hours later.
Olivia enters, followed by Dallas. They've both had too much to drink.
They are both giggling. Dallas is the more drunk of the two.

OLIVIA   Ssh…

DALLAS   *(quite loud)* You ssh…

OLIVIA   But I'm not speaking loudly.

DALLAS   *(still loud)* Neither am I!

OLIVIA   *(sitting on the bed)* I told you not to mix your drinks.

DALLAS   I didn't mix my drinks.

OLIVIA   You did. You had a beer, then wine, then a cider and then a brandy!

DALLAS   *(sitting on the bed)* I know what I had; but I didn't mix them.

OLIVIA   If you know what you had, then you know that you mixed them.

DALLAS   I did not mix them. I had them one after the other. Separately. Each drink had its own glass. Not a single one was mixed with another.

OLIVIA   That's not what mixing drinks means.

DALLAS   Isn't it?

OLIVIA   No.

DALLAS   What does it mean, then?

OLIVIA   It means that you have lots of different drinks over a short period of time which mix in your stomach.

DALLAS   Oh, I see. I never knew that. See; you are a lot cleverer than me.

OLIVIA	*(slurring her s's as z's)* Don't be zo zilly.
DALLAS	What's zilly?
OLIVIA	*(giggling)* You know what I mean.
DALLAS	I don't. Say it again.
OLIVIA	I'm not going to 'coz you'll just take the pizz out of me! *(She hiccups)*
DALLAS	The pizz!?
OLIVIA	*(she hiccups)* Be quiet and get me a glazz of water, pleaze. I've got hiccupz.
DALLAS	*(heading to the bathroom)* I may have mixed my drinks, but I haven't got hiccups!
OLIVIA	They'll go in a min… *(she hiccups)* in a minute.
DALLAS	*(returning with a glass of water)* Your water. But think carefully before you drink it.
OLIVIA	*(she hiccups as she takes the glass)* Why?
DALLAS	Because, if you drink it, it will mix with the wine in your stomach and you will also become a mixer of drinks!
OLIVIA	Don't be zilly. *(She hiccups)* Water doesn't count. *(She drinks some water)* Only alcoholic drinks.
DALLAS	*(sitting down)* Oh, I see. I suppose that makes sense.
OLIVIA	*(taking a few deep breaths)* There. All gone. *(She places the glass on the bedside table)*
DALLAS	I wish my hiccups went that easily. I usually have to stand on my head and things.
OLIVIA	Let's hope you don't get any hiccups tonight, then, as I don't think you'll be up for headstands!
DALLAS	Probably not.

OLIVIA You're not compos mentis.

DALLAS I'd probably agree with you, if I knew what that meant.

They both lay back on the bed with their heads propped up by pillows

OLIVIA *(trying to seem sober)* Did you enjoy your meal?

DALLAS It was alright. I think I'd have preferred fish and chips though.

OLIVIA I did say that diving straight in to a seafood platter might have been a bit too much. Seeing as you'd never tried any of the individual elements before.

DALLAS I know. But, you see, I was thinking that if I ever ran my own fish and chip shop, I could offer other seafood; besides cod and stuff.

OLIVIA That's a good idea.

DALLAS So, I thought I should know what they taste like, if I'm going to put it on the menu.

OLIVIA Makes sound business sense. So, what do you reckon?

DALLAS That I've got a bit of a stomach ache, so I'll let you know in the morning.

OLIVIA Oh dear. Not too bad, is it.

DALLAS Not at the moment.

OLIVIA Good. *(Trying to be sexy, but struggling through drunkenness)* Because I've got plans...

DALLAS *(Not twigging the sexy advance)* So have I.

Crossed wires ensue

OLIVIA Ooo... what plans do you have?

DALLAS That I want to keep trying new things.

OLIVIA Mmm...sounds nice. Like what?

DALLAS	Skate.
OLIVIA	Skate?
DALLAS	Uh-huh.
OLIVIA	Ok. Not sure how that'd work, but I think I've had too much to drink for that. Might get arrested; drunk in charge!
DALLAS	*(not really listening, but just listing seafood)* Plaice.
OLIVIA	Here's fine.
DALLAS	Winkles.
OLIVIA	Plural?
DALLAS	Scallops.
OLIVIA	Ooo… you'll have to show me that one!
DALLAS	*(refocusing on Olivia)* Loads of things.
OLIVIA	*(starting to get hold of Dallas)* Mmm… what shall we start with?
DALLAS	*(extracting himself from Olivia)* I think I'll start with going to the bathroom.
OLIVIA	Ok. You get ready in there and I'll get in bed.

Dallas exits to the bathroom holding his stomach and gently groaning. Olivia slips off a few items of clothing and gets into bed. Dallas returns

OLIVIA	You ok?
DALLAS	*(trying to brave it out)* Yes, I think so.
OLIVIA	Stomach ache still?
DALLAS	Yes, but I'm sure it'll pass.
OLIVIA	*(patting the bed)* You getting in?

DALLAS *(searching in his bag)* Yes; but I've just remembered something. *(Dallas extracts two candles from his bag)* Da daa!

OLIVIA Oh, Dallas, how lovely!

DALLAS *(places one candle on his side of the bed)* One for me. *(He walks round to the other side of the bed)* And one for you! I'll just turn the main light off.

Dallas also has a lighter and he heads to the door to turn off the main light

OLIVIA Don't you think you should light them before you turn the big light off?

DALLAS No. It'll be fine. More romantic this way.

Dallas turns the light off. The room is plunged into darkness. Dallas stubs his toe on the bed/bedside table

DALLAS Ow!

OLIVIA *(turning on her bedside lamp)* Oh, Dallas, are you alright?

DALLAS *(sitting on the floor, rubbing his toes)* Stubbed me toe.

OLIVIA I didn't think lighting them in the dark was a good idea.

DALLAS Even when you're drunk you're cleverer than me.

OLIVIA That's because you're also drunk! Now give me the lighter and I'll light them whilst you get into bed.

DALLAS *(standing up and handing the lighter over)* I think I'll just pop to the loo one more time.

Dallas heads to the bathroom

OLIVIA *(calling)* You are still using the bath, aren't you?

DALLAS *(calling)* Yes, I am. But I might have to find a proper loo soon.

Olivia lights the candles and settles down

OLIVIA   *(calling)* Do you think it's ok having candles?

DALLAS   *(calling)* I should think so, why?

OLIVIA   Because there might be smoke alarms or something.

DALLAS   Are the candles smoking?

OLIVIA   No.

DALLAS   We'll be alright, then.

It goes quiet for a bit. Olivia plays with the candle, maybe playing with the wax. She starts to make a few shadow puppets, then yawns and snuggles down a bit. She drifts off to sleep

A moment

DALLAS   *(calling in a stage whisper)* Olivia…Olivia… I think I'm going to be sick… Olivia! *(He crawls in from the bathroom on all fours)* Olivia…I need something to be sick in…I can't do it in the bath… I need something! *(He crawls round the room, picks up the wicker paper basket, shakes his head and puts it back down. He then crawls round to Olivia's side of the bed, rummages through her bag and extracts a sanitary bag. As he kneels up, he notices the candle Olivia has fiddled with)* Blimey; that is a bit smoky, that one! *(He then crawls back to the bathroom)*

Sound of Dallas being sick offstage. A moment, then he returns holding the bag of sick

DALLAS   Olivia. Are you still asleep? I can't work out what to do with this! Olivia, what shall I do with this? Olivia?

He spies the window (front of stage) and looks out. He sees a bin outside

Ah! A bin. Now, if I can just…

He opens the window, looks out, and takes a couple of practice swings with the bag. Suddenly, the loud sound of a smoke/fire alarm rings out just as he's on his actual throw

DALLAS   Olivia!

The alarm causes Dallas's final throw to falter. As his arm comes forward to launch the bag (towards the auditorium) lights quickly cut to black out

Scene 4

The same, next morning, Sunday. The room is empty with the usual mess of strewn duvet, etc. The candles have gone. A moment. Megan and Trish enter carrying their usual paraphernalia.

TRISH *(sniffing the air)* Got it!

MEGAN You sure?

TRISH You know my nose, Megan, recognises 99.9% of smells in three seconds.

MEGAN 'Coz I thought it was number 17.

TRISH Nope. Someone had just had a quick ciggy in 17. The fire alarm was definitely set off in this room.

MEGAN *(starting to change the bed and sniffing the air a little)* What are you getting then, Trish?

TRISH How about you tell me what you're getting, Megan?

MEGAN Me? Oh, you know me, Trish. I just make the beds. You're the one with the nose.

TRISH True. But it's about time we trained you up. So, take in a big sniff and tell me what you get.

MEGAN Ok. *(Taking a big sniff)* Erm…ooo…I'm not sure.

TRISH Go on. You must have got something.

MEGAN Well, it wasn't very pleasant. I think I can smell sick.

TRISH Oh, yes. There's the smell of sick coming from the bathroom. Besides that?

MEGAN Oh, right. I hadn't really got the sick smell until then… *(sniffing again)* Wax?

TRISH Well done, Megan. Wax, with a hint of cinnamon, quite a nice candle actually, someone was trying to make a bit of an effort… *(heading to what was Olivia's bedside table and poking the hard wax)* and here is quite

	literally the hard evidence.
MEGAN	*(marvelling at Trish before resuming the bed-making)* It's like changing beds with Sherlock Holmes, working with you, Trish.
TRISH	I'll take that as a compliment, Megan.

They continue to make the bed

MEGAN	Will it help if we tell management which room set off the fire alarm.
TRISH	Not really. I might be able to get another squeegee out of them, though.
MEGAN	Worth a shot.
TRISH	That's what I thought. Right, you finish off here; I think I need to check the bathroom. *(She exits to the bathroom)*
MEGAN	Ok.

A moment, then Trish returns

MEGAN	And?
TRISH	Spotless.
MEGAN	Again?
TRISH	Yes.
MEGAN	What, even with the smell of sick?
TRISH	Must've flushed it away.
MEGAN	Oh.
TRISH	*(Pause)* Hang on.
MEGAN	What?
TRISH	I've just had a thought.

MEGAN	Oh, yes?
TRISH	About the sick.
MEGAN	What about it?
TRISH	Well; didn't you hear?
MEGAN	Hear what?
TRISH	The night porter had two people reporting sickness overnight.
MEGAN	Really?
TRISH	And Gary thinks they both had the seafood platter.
MEGAN	My word!
TRISH	Three seafood platters were served last night. If those other two are confirmed as seafood platter eaters; then I think we can assume the third one was from this room.
MEGAN	Yes. I suppose we can.
TRISH	Probably got salmonella.
MEGAN	Probably.
TRISH	All hell was let loose here last night, you know.
MEGAN	It sounds like it.
TRISH	First the fire alarm evacuation; then the two reports of sickness and did you hear about Chef?
MEGAN	No; what about him?
TRISH	Well, according to Gary, Chef left really late last night due to everything going on.
MEGAN	Right.
TRISH	And as he was heading out, the night porter told him of the two reports of sickness.

MEGAN Oh dear.

TRISH Which really wound him up because he thought the night porter was accusing him.

MEGAN Oh, no! Who was on duty last night?

TRISH Old Terry.

MEGAN Oh, well, we all know old Terry wouldn't accuse anyone of anything.

TRISH Exactly! But, with a fuming Chef leaving the hotel, you wouldn't believe what happened next!

MEGAN What!?

TRISH As Gary was getting into his car, he says he saw Chef remove something from the bonnet of his car.

MEGAN Remove something? Remove what?

TRISH Well, from what Gary could see, it looked like a bag of something. Maybe a bag of dog poo which someone had thrown on the bonnet of his car.

MEGAN Oh, that's disgusting.

TRISH I know, and I'm now thinking that it wasn't a bag of dog poo but a bag of sick thrown from this window.

MEGAN You're joking!

TRISH *(heading towards the window)* I wish I was, Megan, I wish I was. *(Pointing out of the window)* But that is where Chef usually parks his car.

MEGAN *(joining Trish at the window)* So it is. *(Pause)* He hasn't had that GTI long, has he?

TRISH No.

MEGAN And it's white.

TRISH Yes.

MEGAN   Oh dear, oh dear.

TRISH   And the last thing Gary heard Chef say was that that's it; he's never coming back!

MEGAN   My word!

TRISH   So, we'll just have to see what happens, won't we?

MEGAN   Yes. What a night! *(Pause. Pointing to the bathroom)* What have you done about the smell of sick in there?

TRISH   *(holding up a can of air freshener)* I just gave a liberal spray of our fruity friend here, and job's a good 'un! Finished the bed, Dr Watson?

MEGAN   I certainly have, Mr Holmes. It was elementary!

TRISH   Yes. Or, *(she sprays the air freshener and sniffs it)* lemonentary!

They both laugh as they exit

Lights fade to black out

Scene 5

Later the same day. Peter and Claire enter. Both early 70s. Claire enters first, carrying two small cases. Peter follows holding his oil-covered hands in the air.

CLAIRE Now, don't touch anything Peter.

PETER I'm not touching anything, Claire.

CLAIRE *(putting the cases down)* Straight through to the bathroom with you.

PETER *(heading off)* Righto!

CLAIRE Hang on. Let me get the bathroom door for you.

PETER Righto!

CLAIRE *(she does this and returns to sit on the bed. Calling)* Alright in there?

PETER Yes.

CLAIRE Are the towels white?

PETER Sorry?

CLAIRE The towels. At the moment are they white?

PETER Erm, yes. At the moment the towels are white.

CLAIRE Well; can we keep them that way?

PETER Sorry?

CLAIRE I said can we keep the towels white. As in *(in some sort of tune)* 'soap and water wash dirt away; towels will last another day!'

PETER Righto.

Claire picks up her handbag

PETER *(singing from the bathroom)* 'Soap and water wash dirt away; towels will last another day!'

Claire shakes her head and looks around for a phone

CLAIRE Oh; no phone! *(She starts to look through her bag for her mobile phone. Retrieving her mobile)* I'll have to use my mobile. *(She punches a number into it whilst Peter continues to repeat the rhyme quietly in the bathroom. Into phone)* Hello Andrew. It's your mum.... No only just got here.... I know.... Took over an hour longer.... Something went wrong under the bonnet and your dad insisted on fixing it.... I told him that we should have taken the Nissan, but it's a Sunday and you know what he's like about using the Sunday car on a Sunday.... He's currently getting all the oil and muck off his hands in the bathroom.... Listen.... *(She holds the phone up)* Yes.... He remembers that one.... Are Sue, Samuel and Eleanor ok? .... Yes, well, suggesting we came back to the old hotel was a lovely idea. Yes; same room, 27. It had an actual name, this room, when we honeymooned here; can't remember it though. *(Looking around for the first time)* Oh, yes, I see what you mean when you thought the hotel room must have aged. It has! Yes, well, I suppose it comes to us all; even bricks and mortar! *(She laughs)* We really enjoyed looking after your two. But it has taken it out of your dad quite a bit.... But I'm sure the break will do him good. It might bring back some memories.... I'll call you when we get home tomorrow.... Ok, bye for now.... Bye. *(She hangs up)*

Peter enters from the bathroom holding one clean hand in the air. With the other hand he is holding up a white towel

PETER *(in rhyme)* 'When your hands are clean, and your towel is too; you know that you've done the best that you can do!'

CLAIRE *(patting the bed next to her)* Well done, Peter. Come and sit down.

Peter sits

I've just phoned Andrew.

PETER Oh, yes?

CLAIRE I do worry about him.

PETER Yes.

CLAIRE Well, I worry about both of them.

PETER Yes. *(He continues to listen carefully)*

CLAIRE We started out young, didn't we? We were fit and able to cope with four children... just. Andrew and Susan met so much later in life. Giving birth to twins in your forties must be such a strain; both physically and mentally. *(Pause)* We had tough moments didn't we... four children before we were thirty... including Michael.

PETER *(quietly)* Michael...

CLAIRE But we made it through, didn't we?

PETER Yes.

CLAIRE We've been, on the whole, happy, haven't we?

PETER Definitely.

CLAIRE They'll be alright, won't they?

PETER Who?

CLAIRE Andrew and Susan. They'll be alright?

PETER Of course.

CLAIRE They'll be as happy as us.

PETER Of course they will. They've got each other.

CLAIRE Yes. That's right. They've got each other.

Pause.

CLAIRE (*Trying to lift the mood*) Anyway; Andrew says we should have come in the Nissan.

PETER No, no, no. It's a Sunday.

CLAIRE I know it's a Sunday. But that old car isn't very reliable, is it?

PETER She, Claire, not it.

CLAIRE Sorry. She.

PETER She got us here, didn't she?

CLAIRE Only just.

PETER She still got us here.

CLAIRE Yes. But I do find her difficult to drive.

PETER She still got us here.

CLAIRE Yes.

PETER I can drive her home again.

CLAIRE No, no, Peter. No more driving for you. Doctor's orders.

PETER (*a little downbeat*) Oh.

CLAIRE You remember why, don't you?

PETER Erm, no.

CLAIRE Ikea. Last year.

PETER Erm.

CLAIRE The car park.

PETER Ah, yes.

CLAIRE You remember now?

93

PETER Yes.

CLAIRE I thought you would, seeing as it's to do with the car.

PETER I got the dent out of her.

CLAIRE Yes. You did very well.

PETER And Michael helped me.

CLAIRE *(placing her hand on Peter's)* No, no, Andrew helped you. Not Michael.

PETER Michael didn't help?

CLAIRE No, no. Michael didn't help. Just Andrew.

PETER Righto.

CLAIRE *(taking hold of one of Peter's hands which has a plaster on its little finger)* Now then. Let's take that dirty plaster off your little finger and get a nice fresh one on there. *(She does this whilst talking)* We don't want that nasty infection to get any worse, do we?

PETER No.

CLAIRE No. I don't know how it came back again. I thought we'd got rid of it.

PETER Yes.

CLAIRE *(finishing off)* There we go!

Pause

PETER Dinner?

CLAIRE Ah, now, do you remember when we signed in we were told that the dining room was closed this evening?

PETER Why?

CLAIRE Well, they weren't very clear, but I think the chef's ill, or something. But it's probably a good thing as we know what you can sometimes be like in a crowded room, don't we?

PETER Yes.

CLAIRE So they ordered a pizza for us and said they'd send it up when it was delivered.

PETER Righto. *(Pause)* Pepperoni?

CLAIRE Yes. Pepperoni for Peter!

PETER Perfect!

Peter starts to scratch the plastered finger

CLAIRE Is that finger feeling sore again?

PETER A bit.

CLAIRE Well; getting it covered in oil probably hasn't helped.

PETER No.

CLAIRE Right, well, what would you like to do before the pizza arrives?

PETER Erm, read, I think.

CLAIRE Ok. Did you bring your book?

PETER No.

CLAIRE Well that's going to make reading a bit difficult, isn't it?

PETER *(spying the Bible)* I'll read this.

CLAIRE Really?

PETER Yes. *(He sits up by the headboard and opens the Bible)*

CLAIRE Do you have your reading glasses?

PETER Erm, no.

CLAIRE Well, that's going to make reading even more difficult, isn't it?

PETER Yes.

CLAIRE *(joining Peter by the headboard)* Give it here. I'll read it to you.

PETER *(handing the Bible over)* Ok.

CLAIRE Shall we go random. Like we normally do when faced with a big book?

PETER Yes.

CLAIRE Ok. *(She opens the Bible)* Right. It looks like we've got Genesis I. Good place to start. *(Reading)* 'Then God said, "Behold, I have given you every plant yielding seed that is on the surface of all the earth, and every tree which has fruit yielding seed; it shall be food for you."' Oh, food. God must know we're hungry, eh, Peter?

PETER Yes.

CLAIRE Let's try another. *(Skips forward a few pages. Reading)* Ok. Genesis 18: 'So Abraham hurried into the tent to Sarah, and said, "Quickly, prepare three measures of fine flour, knead it and make bread cakes."' *(Surprised)* Oh! More food. *(Turning the Bible at an angle)* What does this say? *(Reading)* 'Make sure you put chocolate spread on those bread cakes and not Marmite.' My word! That's a bit strange.

PETER Yes.

CLAIRE Mind. They probably get all sorts staying in here. *(Flicking through the Bible once more)* Right let's try here. Ecclesiastes 9: 'Go then, eat your bread in happiness and drink your wine with a cheerful heart; for God has already approved your works.' Well! It can't all be food in here, can it?

PETER   No.

CLAIRE   No.

PETER   It's making me hungry.

CLAIRE   Yes, me too. I'm sure the pizza won't be long. *(Turning to the bedside table)* Oh, of course.

PETER   What?

CLAIRE   Just remembered that there isn't a phone.

PETER   Oh.

CLAIRE   I was going to phone down to reception to see how long the pizza would be. But it can't be long now.

PETER   No.

CLAIRE   Right. One more try to find a bit in the Bible which isn't going to make our tummies rumble, Peter.

PETER   Ok.

CLAIRE   *(turning the page)* Ecclesiastes 12: 'Remember also your Creator in the days of your youth, before the evil days come and the years draw near of which you will say, "I have no pleasure in them"; before the sun and the light and the moon and the stars are darkened and the clouds return after the rain, in the day when the keepers of the house tremble, and the strong men are bent, and the grinders cease because they are few, and those who look through the windows are dimmed, and the doors on the street are shut – when the sound of the grinding is low, and one rises up at the sound of a bird, and all the daughters of song are brought low – they are afraid also of what is high, and terrors are in the way; the almond tree blossoms, the grasshopper drags itself along, and desire fails, because man is going to his eternal home, and the mourners go about the streets – before the silver cord is snapped, or the golden bowl is broken, or the pitcher is shattered at the fountain, or the wheel broken at the cistern, and the dust returns to the earth as it was, and the spirit returns to God who gave it. Vanity of vanities, says the Preacher; all is vanity.'

During the above, Peter has taken an oily hanky from his pocket and dabbed his eyes. Claire closes the Bible and looks lovingly at Peter. A moment

CLAIRE   Do you recognise this room, Peter?

PETER   *(looking around)* Erm, no.

CLAIRE   I mean, I thought it would have changed too much for either of us to remember, but it's very much the same.

PETER   Oh.

CLAIRE   There was a trouser press over there, behind the door. Now, that was a real mod-con back then!

PETER   Right.

CLAIRE   And all the furniture and fittings were solid and new.

PETER   Yes.

CLAIRE   And the wallpaper was beautiful.

PETER   Yes.

CLAIRE   All beautiful, bright flowers everywhere. The room was named after the flower and I can't, for the life of me, remember the name.

PETER   No.

CLAIRE   But I remember everything else.

PETER   Yes.

CLAIRE   Do you recognise this room *at all*, Peter?

PETER   *(looking around once more)* I don't think so.

CLAIRE   *(taking his hand)* We spent some of our honeymoon here.

PETER Did we?

CLAIRE Yes.

PETER With Michael?

CLAIRE *(trying not to get upset)* No, no, Peter. Not with Michael. It was before Michael.

PETER Righto.

Pause

Claire gets up from the bed and walks to the window

CLAIRE *(looking out of the window)* We got married in the little church on the… oh; you can't see it any more. New buildings in the way.

PETER Oh dear.

CLAIRE Then we walked across the fields to here. *(Looking out again)* The size of that road out there I doubt you could walk to here from any direction without being mown down.

PETER Yes.

CLAIRE Do you remember carrying me over the threshold into the hotel.

PETER No.

CLAIRE *(tears are welling up. Through the next the tears start to trickle down her face)* Then we came up here and you carried me over the threshold into this room and you laid me on the bed and… *(it's all become too much)*

Peter is looking around the room. Then he stops and stares at Claire.

Pause

PETER The Turkish Rose room.

CLAIRE	Pardon?
PETER	*(pointing at the wall)* The Turkish Rose room.
CLAIRE	*(in disbelief)* My God, George! You remembered the name of the room!
PETER	George? I'm not George. I'm Peter.
CLAIRE	*(completely taken aback by what she's just said)* What!? Sorry. Of course, Peter. I don't know where that came from!
PETER	You ok?
CLAIRE	I think so, Peter, thank you. It's just been a bit of a long day.
PETER	Yes.
CLAIRE	*(recovering her composure)* But, you remembered the name of the room.
PETER	Yes.
CLAIRE	*(looking at the wall)* They're all faded, but you're right. The room was once covered in beautiful pink roses. The Turkish Rose room!

Claire sits on the bed next to Peter and holds his hand. Peter spies the tears on Claire's cheeks and reaches into his pocket and removes the oily looking hanky once more and offers it to her

PETER	*(noticing the state of the hanky as he hands it to Claire)* Erm, sorry. It's all I have.
CLAIRE	*(accepting the hanky)* That's fine, Peter. Thank you. *(She carefully dabs her eyes)*

The moment is suddenly broken by a knock at the door

PETER	*(excitedly)* Pizza!

CLAIRE	*(not quite so excited)* Yes, pizza. *(She goes to the door, opens it, and receives a pizza box)* Thank you. *(She returns to the bed)* Now; we can eat it here as long as you try not to get any crumbs on the bed.
PETER	Ok. No crumbs.
CLAIRE	No crumbs.
PETER	No crumbs.
CLAIRE	*(opening the box)* Lovely pepperoni pizza for Peter.
PETER	Mmmm. Can we sing?
CLAIRE	Really?
PETER	Yes, please.
CLAIRE	Ok. *(Lifting up the pizza box)* Ready?
PETER	Ready.
CLAIRE	*(offering the pizza to Peter. Singing to melody of 'Ode to Joy')* Take a piece of pizza, Peter, pepperoni piece for you. Take just one to start with, Peter, then maybe you can have two.
PETER	Thank you. *(He takes a slice and starts to eat)*
CLAIRE	*(continuing to sing)* Take a piece of pizza, Peter, pepperoni piece for you. Take just one to start with, Peter, then maybe you can have two. *(Tears start to roll once more down Claire's cheeks)*

Throughout the above lights fade to black out

The End

Printed in Great Britain
by Amazon